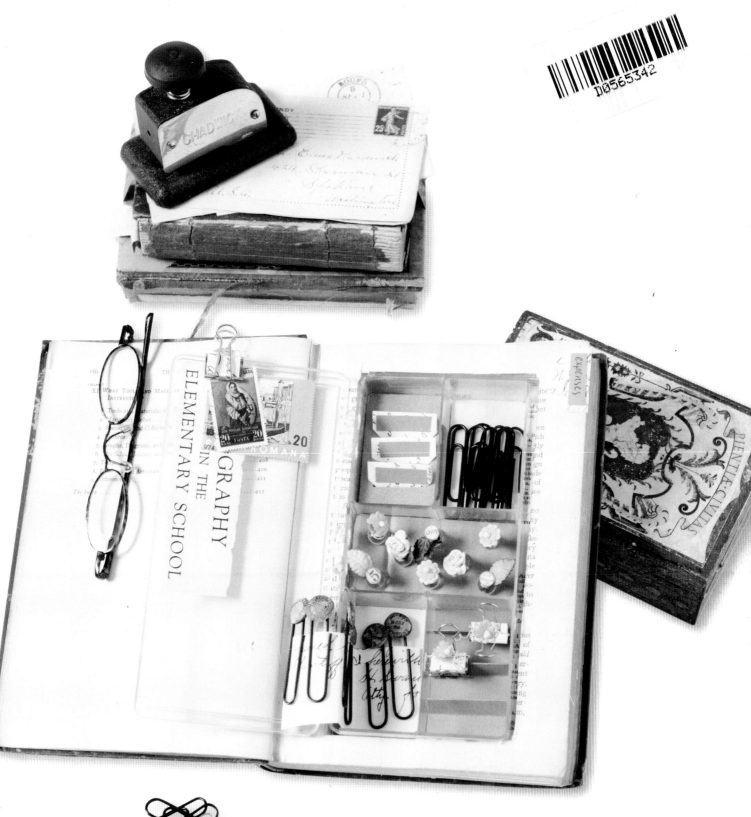

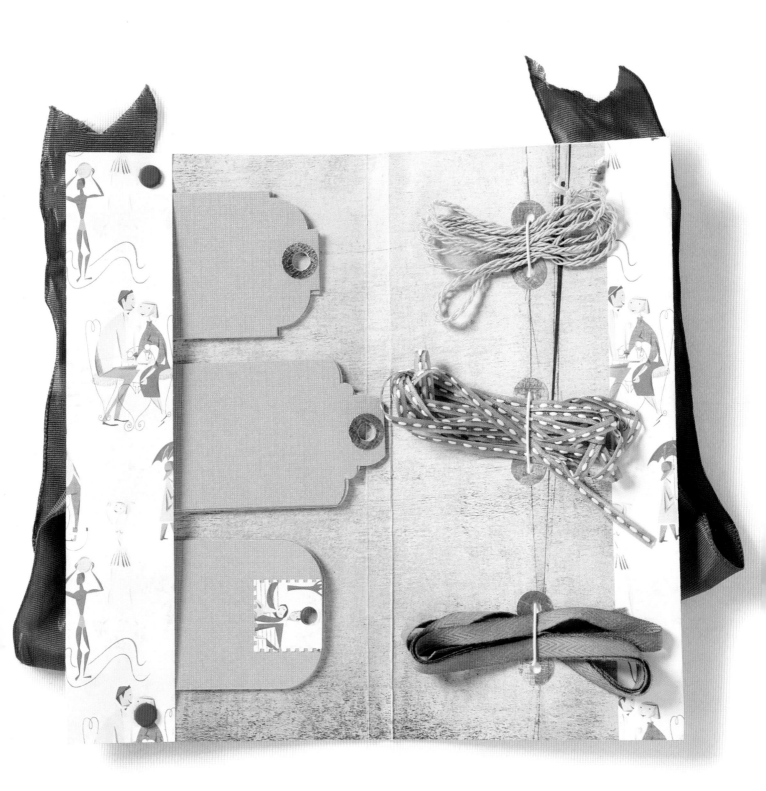

Paper Art Workshop

HANDMADE GIFTS

Stylish Ideas for Journals, Stationery, and More

GLOUCESTER MASSACHUSETTS

QUARRY BOOKS

jennifer francis bitto, linda blinn, jenn mason [THE MIXED MEDIUMS]

First published in the United States of America by
Quarry Books, a member of
Quayside Publishing Group
33 Commercial Street
Gloucester, Massachusetts 01930-5089
Telephone: (978) 282-9590
Fax: (978) 283-2742
www.rockpub.com

Library of Congress Cataloging-in-Publication Data
Bitto, Jennifer Francis.
    Handmade gifts : stylish ideas for journals, stationery, and more / Jennifer Francis Bitto,
Linda Blinn, Jenn Mason.
      p.   cm.
    ISBN 1-59253-286-1 (pbk.)
    1. Handicraft. 2. Paperwork. I. Blinn, Linda. II. Mason, Jenn. III. Title.
TT157.B56 2006
745.54—dc22   2006007258
                                                             CIP

ISBN-13: 978-1-59253-286-5
ISBN-10: 1-59253-286-1

10 9 8 7 6 5 4 3 2 1

Design: Yee Design
Illustrations and templates: Jenn Mason

Printed in Singapore

The Mixed Mediums
AUTHORS, ARTISTS, TEACHERS

Jennifer Francis Bitto
Linda Blinn
Jenn Mason

www.theMixedMediums.com

CONTENTS

Introduction **8**

Tools and Supplies **10**

CHAPTER 1: The Traveler

Traveling Light: The Perfect Handmade Journal **14**

Your Passport Please: Document Holder **16**

Nothing to Declare: Luggage Tag **19**

Frequent Flier: Traveling Artist Portfolio **20**

Leftovers **24**

CHAPTER 2: The Paper Pusher

Magnetic Personality: Metal Message Board **29**

Collage Under Glass: Paperweights **30**

Calling All Cards: Business Card Holder **33**

Classy Office Supplies: New Use for an Old Book **37**

Leftovers **40**

CHAPTER 3: The Chef

Chef's Collection: Kitchen Journal **44**

Arty-Chokes: Kitschy Culinary Art **49**

Recipe Management: Stylish Clipboards **50**

Leftovers **54**

CHAPTER 4: The Girlfriend

East Meets West: Origami Writing Set **58**

Flea Market Style: French Flower Buckets **62**

Perfect Posies: Paper Flowers **66**

Designs from Nature: Journal Necklace **71**

A Best Seller: The Button Book **75**

Leftovers **78**

CHAPTER 5: The Giver

Beautifully Composed: Composition-Book Cards 82

The Big Easy: 20-Minute Cards 86

Pick a Tag, Any Tag: Gift Tag Folios 88

Showing Your Sentiments: May I Have a Word? Garland 92

Rah! Rah! Rah!: Gift Bag Pennants 94

Supreme Makeover: Well-Dressed Office Supplies 97

Purposeful Pockets: Cards with a Message 98

Fold, Cut, and Wrap: Gift Garlands 101

Leftovers 102

Templates.. 104

Clip Art 114

Product Manufacturers by Project.................... 120

Out and About with the Mixed Mediums 122

Product Resources 124

Supply Contributors............................... 125

About the Authors 127

Acknowledgments 128

INTRODUCTION

Paper art and personalized gifts are wrapped up together and beautifully presented in this book by us, three artists who became friends. Our shared escapades to find unusual materials for gifts resulted in innovative paper projects we designed and gave to each other. This combination of art, adventure, and friendship became the catalyst for this book.

While sitting on the floor of an antique store pawing through old books and ephemera for gift ideas, our girl talk began morphing into something that sounded like a table of contents for a gift book. Soon we were exploring the broader topics of a series of books (we had moved on to architectural salvage), and by the time we found vintage clothing we had more ideas than Jenn could enter into her PDA and still shop.

As a tribute to our diverse blend of backgrounds, techniques, and design aesthetics, we agreed that calling ourselves The Mixed Mediums reflected our all-inclusive approach to paper art. The name also gives a wink to how we each "channel" our ideas in different ways. The result is our first book, an eclectic slate of chapters, each for a different type of person in your life.

The many things we learned about ourselves and each other as artists, women, and friends are part of the story. We hope you enjoy that part along with the exciting ideas for paper gifts made for travelers, paper pushers, chefs, girlfriends, and givers.

And, if you are short on time or experience, a section at the end of each chapter, called Leftovers, will have you turning the smallest scraps and extra supplies from the featured projects into easy, breezy embellishments, tags, envelopes, and small books.

Tools and Supplies

If we had only five minutes to grab our favorite art materials, they would include all the items on this list. You might not need every single item, but you will likely have more fun if you have them all!

Basic Tool Kit

The Basic Tool Kit appears throughout the book. It contains the fundamental tools you will need to make the featured projects.

- bone folder
- craft knife
- hole punch
- metal-edge ruler
- scissors
- stylus

Extras

Keep this list with you and pick up some of these supplies when you see them. You will soon have a stash at your fingertips and be ready to craft at a moment's notice.

ADHESIVES

- clear glaze
- Diamond Glaze
- double-stick tape
- gel medium
- gesso
- glue stick
- hook and loop tape (such as Velcro)
- mounting foam tape
- removable tape
- spray adhesive
- stapler
- white glue
- Zots

HARDWARE

- brads
- decorative punches
- decorative-edge scissors
- eyelets
- eyelet setter
- jewelry crimping ends
- jump rings
- lobster clasp
- magnets
- pliers
- post and screw fastener
- wire cutters

EMBELLISHMENTS

- black elastic
- buttons
- collage items such as mailbox stickers, wooden letters, old rulers, magnetic clips, or brass charms
- decorative tape
- epoxy stickers
- glitter
- photo corners
- ribbon
- rub-on letters, words, designs
- rubber stamps
- stickers
- waxed string or twine

Items You'll Need to Make These Specific Projects

PAPER

- acetate transparency
- blank postcards
- canceled postage stamps
- clip art
- decorative papers such as wrapping paper or scrapbook paper
- die-cut letters and shapes
- envelopes—paper, vellum, glassine, coin
- library pockets
- mat board
- old maps
- photographs
- plain-colored card stock
- poster board
- tags—all shapes and sizes
- thin and heavy cardboard
- tissue paper
- vintage papers and ephemera
- watercolor paper

FOR ADDING COLOR

- acrylic paint
- chalkboard paint
- chalks or pastels
- colored pencils and watercolor pencils
- foam brushes
- ink pads
- markers
- metallic foil pens
- paintbrushes

- adhesive CD pockets
- beads
- blank books (composition books in various sizes work well)
- bolts and wing nuts measuring 3" (7.6 cm)
- box measuring 4" x 6" (10.2 x 15.2 cm)
- brass locket
- CD and jewel case
- clear plastic, adhesive-backed container (called a Display Box, made by 3M)
- corrugated cardboard
- cotton or leather cord
- crepe paper
- decorative paper clips
- drill
- faux artichokes
- felt scrap
- file folders (we used black)
- florist tape—green
- florist wire—green
- heat gun
- heat-shrink tubing
- heavyweight paper (at least 100 lb [about 270 gsm])
- iridescent stainless steel acrylic (Golden)
- kitchen drawer knobs and washers
- metal hole punch or hammer and nail
- metal ring

- metal roof flashing on a roll
- paint chips
- paper clips
- paper flowers
- paperweight
- piece of chalk
- plastic box
- plastic sheet protector
- purchased portfolio measuring 12 1/2" x 9 1/2" (31.8 x 24.1 cm)
- pushpins
- recipe cards
- sewing machine
- spiral-bound sketchbook measuring 6" x 4" (15.2 x 10.2 cm)
- small clipboards
- small paper flowers and leaves
- small plastic bags
- small ribbon buckle
- small sewing kit with thread spools, needles, pins, and scissors
- string and button envelope measuring 9" x 4" (22.9 x 10.2 cm)
- trifold portfolio (chipboard or heavy paper)
- vintage book
- white shrink plastic
- wire
- wooden dowels measuring 1/8" (3 mm)

1 THE TRAVELER

In another era, the phrase *traveling in style* might have conjured up images of huge Louis Vuitton trunks being loaded on to a cruise ship, with porters available to transport them to your room. Now, the trunk is more likely a microfiber suitcase that converts to a backpack—and the porter who is going to be carrying it the entire trip is you.

These projects offer a way to travel in style, even if getting there means being stuck in security lines, wedged into an airplane seat, and eating food with an expiration date stamped on the package.

While experimenting with shades of blue and green paint on a huge sheet of rosin paper from the home improvement store, the combination of colors reminded us of a world map. Sometimes hand-painted paper tells *you* what it wants to be: in this case, a cover for a travel journal. And with the ample amount of leftover paper, an entire set of matching travel accessories was born.

The cover for the journal was designed to fit generic composition books. It is removable and durable enough to travel again with a fresh book inside for the next destination. With a matching ID tag, the set is ready to start accruing its own frequent flyer miles.

We all know the joy of spotting our luggage as it arrives on the airport carousel. But in the sea of hundreds of black bags all cloned from the same DNA, is it really the one we checked in with? We have seen a lot of solutions to marking your suitcase and conclude that a colorful, one-of-a-kind luggage tag makes a better statement than duct tape. Add a matching passport cover and a portable artist's kit to the travel collection, and your gift set is ready to fly.

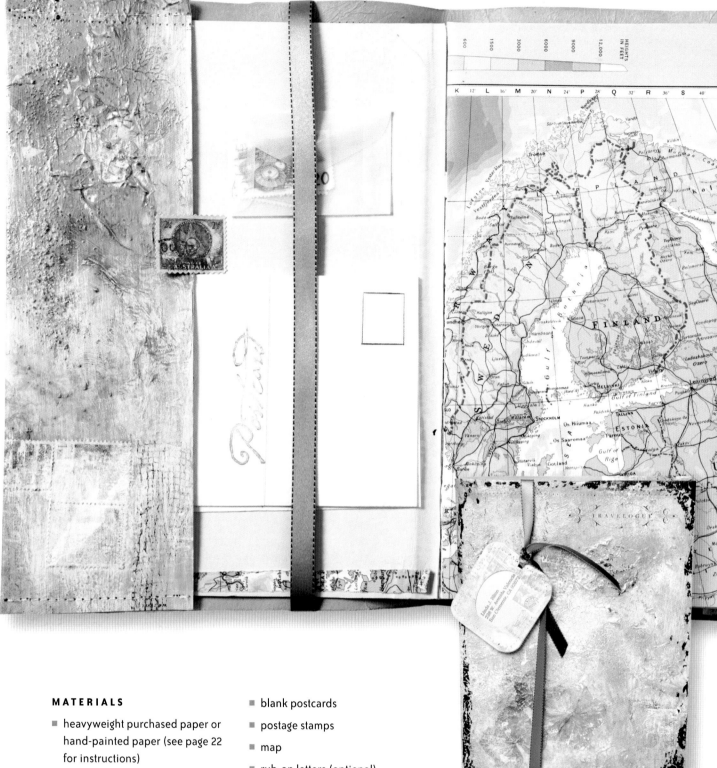

Journal cover

MATERIALS

- heavyweight purchased paper or hand-painted paper (see page 22 for instructions)
- blank book (composition book or journal measuring 7$\frac{1}{2}$" x 10" [19.1 x 25.4 cm])
- glassine envelope
- ribbon
- blank postcards
- postage stamps
- map
- rub-on letters (optional)

TOOLS

- basic tool kit (see page 10)
- sewing machine

The Perfect Handmade Journal

It is said that the journey is the destination. For many, that journey starts the minute they decide to take a trip. This lightweight, durable journal will be a welcome gift for those who wish to record their adventures from beginning to end, whether they are going to an exotic locale or a nearby state.

A thoughtful "gift within a gift" idea is to tuck preaddressed postcards and a supply of stamps into the inside of the journal cover, making it easy for the traveler to stay in touch. Add a pack of pens in different colors and a card made from a map, and wish the recipient bon voyage. (See Leftovers, page 24, if you would like to make an ID tag from the extra supplies used in making gifts for the traveler.)

INSTRUCTIONS

1 Measure the book, adding 4" (10.2 cm) to the width and 1" (2.5 cm) to the height. Cut decorative paper to that measurement.

2 Place the open book on the center of the paper and fold a 2" (5.1 cm) flap over the inside of the front and back covers. Make a crease at the fold.

3 Remove the book. Machine stitch at the top and bottom of each cover flap, 1/4" (6 mm) from the edge.

4 Apply rub-on letters or phrases to the outside of the cover as desired.

5 Open the book and glue another pattern of decorative paper onto the inside front and inside back covers.

6 Glue a map to the front of the first page.

7 Slip the book inside the sewn cover. Place the blank postcards inside the front flap. Fill a glassine envelope with postage stamps and affix to the inside cover.

8 Loop the ribbon around the front cover to help secure postcards and other items in the front flap.

Document Holder

As long as you are sending off the traveler in style, the passport can be dressed up too. With some paper left over from the journal project and a plastic envelope, you can have one ready before the suitcases are packed.

MATERIALS

- heavy paper to match journal (see page 22)
- tissue paper
- brads
- waxed string
- plastic sleeve
- rub-on letters
- canceled postage stamps
- hook and loop tape

TOOLS

- basic tool kit (see page 10)

INSTRUCTIONS

1 Cut a piece of leftover decorated paper measuring 13" x 5" (33 x 12.7 cm). Crinkle the tissue paper, then smooth it out and affix with spray or liquid glue to the undecorated side of the paper.

2 Fold a $1/2$" (1.3 cm) flap on one end. Make another fold $6^{1}/2$" (16.5 cm) from the other end.

3 Use rub-on letters to spell Passport on the front and add canceled postage stamps if desired. Use rub-on borders to highlight the edges.

4 Construct a string and button closure or apply adhesive-back hook and loop tape to the inside of the flap.

5 If using the holder for a passport, place the passport inside and secure the closure.

6 If using the holder for receipts, business cards, stamps, or other items, slide the plastic sleeve inside and secure the closure.

Adapt this project to organize a variety of necessities including receipts, business cards, and stamps. Transform the holder into a pouch by sewing the sides together. In this case, do not attach the plastic envelope to the inside. This enables it to be removed so items can be inserted easily before replacing it in the pouch.

Luggage Tag

This is a gift in itself and one that can be personalized and adapted for many uses—a golf or gym bag, a computer carrying case, a backpack, or even a baby stroller. The luggage tag has four layers: a front, a clear plastic window, personal information or business card, and a back. A strap is attached after the layers are assembled.

MATERIALS

- handmade heavy paper (see page 22) or purchased heavy paper
- acetate transparency
- plain-colored card stock
- post and screw fastener

TOOLS

- basic tool kit (see page 10)
- sewing machine (optional)
- template (see page 105)

INSTRUCTIONS

1 Trace the template on page 105, and cut the front and back of the luggage tag from the paper used in the travel set or another paper of your choice. Cut a 9" x 1^1/2" (22.9 x 3.8 cm) strip from the same paper to be used for the strap.

2 Sew the front and back of the tag together, leaving the top of the tag open for inserting personal information. Cut a 2^1/2" x 3^1/2" (6.4 x 8.9 cm) rectangle from clear plastic or an acetate transparency sheet.

3 Print the personal information onto card stock and cut to 2" x 3^1/2" (5.1 x 8.9 cm). Place the acetate transparency on top of it and slip into the top of the tag. A business card also can be used.

4 To make the strap, fold the long side edges of the strap paper toward the center so they meet in the middle. This will be the underneath side of the strap. Glue down the edges. The strap should measure approximately ^{3}/4" (1.9 cm) wide.

5 Punch a hole in each end of the strap ^{1}/2" (1.3 cm) from the edge. Round the corners with scissors.

6 Punch a hole in the top center of the tag ^{1}/2" (1.3 cm) from the edge as shown in the template.

7 Align the holes in the strap with the hole in the tag and secure with a post and screw fastener.

Traveling Artist Portfolio

The urge to record what you see and experience likely goes all the way back to cave paintings. In the nineteenth century, men and women of the Victorian era applied their writing and artistic abilities to fill their travel journals with words, drawing, and painting. Even now, although most everyone has access to cameras, many travelers prefer to record their experiences in an art journal.

This traveling art portfolio provides a lightweight, packable alternative to purchased kits. We started with a generic (and inexpensive) portfolio from the office supply store and adapted it for a gift. Ours is personalized for a certain friend who uses sketchbooks *and* watercolors, so we included her favorite brands in the portfolio. Tailor yours to your favorite traveling artist.

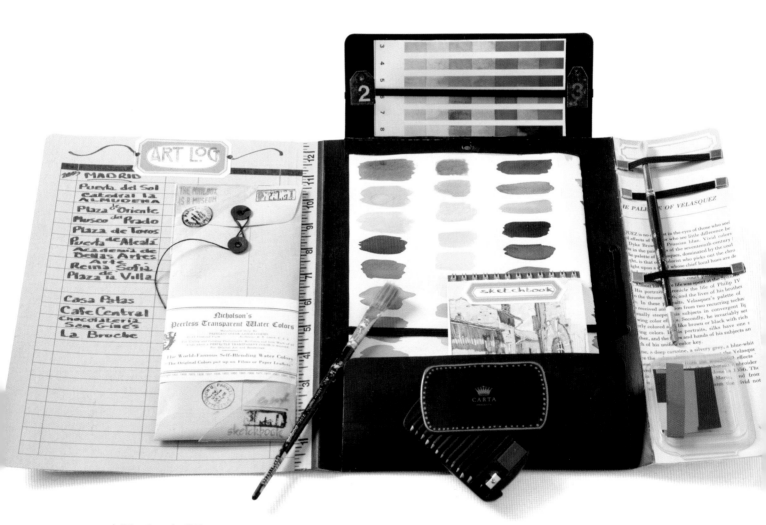

MATERIALS

- purchased portfolio measuring $12^{1}/2$" x $9^{1}/2$" (31.8 x 24.1 cm)
- map of destination
- spiral-bound sketchbook measuring 6" x 4" (15.2 x 10.2 cm) (optional add-on)
- string and button envelope measuring 9" x 4" (22.9 x 10.2 cm)
- black elastic, $^{1}/4$" (6 mm) wide, approximately 1 yard (91.4 cm) long
- decorative brads
- black acrylic paint (we used chalkboard paint)
- paintbrushes
- watercolor paper
- clear plastic adhesive-back container
- small box of colored pencils
- text from an old art book
- Peerless Transparent Water Colors book
- measuring tape
- rub-on letters
- adhesive labels
- copper pen
- hook and loop tape

TOOLS

- basic tool kit (see page 10)

INSTRUCTIONS

1 Affix a map or other image to the front of the portfolio.

2 Paint the center panel and flaps black.

3 Cut a length of black elastic to fit around the top flap and affix with brads.

4 Cut a length of black elastic and affix across the back panel, approximately 4" (10.2 cm) from the bottom edge. This will hold the watercolor paper.

5 Apply adhesive-back hook and loop tape to the bottom of the colored pencil box and affix to the bottom flap. Highlight the edges with a copper pen if desired.

6 Cover the right-hand flap with text from an old art book.

7 Secure three strips of black elastic horizontally with brads on the right-hand flap. Place the watercolor brushes behind the elastic.

8 Affix an adhesive-back container at the bottom of the flap to hold the watercolor strips or water.

9 Attach a string and button envelope on the far right side of the inside cover. (We used 3M Giant Photo Corners.)

10 Stamp the corners with permanent ink (such as StazOn).

11 Place a Peerless Transparent Water Colors book in the envelope.

12 Embellish with adhesive labels, rub-on letters, and measuring tape.

Supersize and Personalize Your Paper

Transform ordinary paper that comes on large rolls with various surface treatments, and open up the possibilities for innovative projects. The samples shown are made using rolls of paper from home improvement and art supply stores. They include heavy brown kraft paper, red rosin paper (used by the construction industry), Art Kraft duo-finish paper (from Pacon), and large sheets of solid color paper with a weight of 100 lb to 140 lb (219 to 307 gsm).

The Advantages of Painting Your Own Supersized Papers:

- gives you the opportunity to design bigger projects or a set of matching projects such as the travel set in this chapter
- increases the strength of the paper by using various paints, gel medium, and other products that add texture to the paper
- maximizes your time by painting multiple sheets in one sitting
- achieves the exact color and design that might not be available with purchased papers
- uses up products that you have on hand
- helps you develop new painting techniques and color schemes
- personalizes the paper with a gift project in mind
- gives you the opportunity to exercise your large arm muscles with broad brushstrokes and make a mess!

Studio Tip

When working on large sheets of paper, remind yourself that the sheet will not been seen as a whole composition. You will have a tendency to try to make it look like a finished piece but it just needs to be consistent in color and texture. The big surprise comes when you cut it into pieces for your projects. Each section will look entirely different while still sharing the same color scheme and surface techniques. It is always a pleasant surprise when your least favorite areas look stunning when seen apart from the rest of the sheet.

SAMPLE A: *Used in the travel set on page 14*

1. Apply a coat of white gesso to a large sheet of 140 lb (approximately 307 gsm) paper.

2. Apply heavy gel medium with a palette knife to areas of the paper for texture and strength. It is not necessary to cover the entire surface. For a variation, add coarse pumice gel to create a gritty texture. If desired, embed dried flowers or paper ephemera in the heavy gel medium at this stage. Let dry.

3. Apply one color of acrylic paint to the areas of textured gel and apply another color (or colors) to fill in the areas between. (The samples here use light blue and light green.) Let dry.

4. Using a dry brush, lightly apply gesso to the surface to unify the colors.

5. Additional painting techniques such as splattering can be done to add texture and interest.

SAMPLE B: *A folded 140 lb paper book cover.*

1. Apply a layer of gesso.

2. Brush on a layer of paint, working in one direction.

3. When dry, lightly brush on another color in the opposite direction.

4. Finish with additional surface techniques such as stamping, splattering, or collaging.

SAMPLE C

1. Paint the red rosin paper first with gesso and then an aqua-colored acrylic paint. Let dry.

2. Lightly brush with gel medium and affix sheer fabric to the surface. Let dry.

3. Machine stitch to highlight the pattern in the fabric.

SAMPLE D

1. Paint the red rosin paper with gesso. Let dry.

2. Use spray glue to affix tissue paper, sheet music, and ephemera over the entire surface.

3. Apply a coat of gel medium over the collaged papers.

4. Use gold webbing spray in several areas to add texture and unify the papers.

SAMPLE E: *For use as a kitchen wall accessory*

1. Paint the red rosin paper with gesso. Let dry.

2. On a paper plate, squeeze dime-sized amounts of the shades of red and orange fluid acrylic paints. Add a few drops of water to thin paints.

3. Using a paintbrush, apply the colors randomly and in different directions to cover the entire surface. Paint quickly and freely. Let dry.

4. Use a black calligraphy marker to draw tomatoes on the surface. Stamp the word tomato vertically with large alphabet stamps. Collage a recipe using tomatoes onto the surface under the drawing.

SAMPLE F

1. Cover the sheet with gesso and let dry.

2. Add irregular layers of acrylic paint.

3. Cover the painted surface with patterns of rubber stamping, collaging, and die-cut objects.

Leftovers

Quick Ideas for Using Your Scraps

Each time you finish a paper art project, you will likely have some leftover materials. Don't stash leftover paper in drawers or throw it away—create more stuff!

1

May I See Your ID?

This ID tag will get you name recognition.

① Read the instructions for making the luggage tag on page 19.

② Use the template on page 105 to trace the shape for the smaller luggage tag, omitting the strap.

③ Punch a hole at the top and insert a ribbon. Tie it to the travel journal or anything else you want to claim as yours.

Ornamental Photographs

This photograph hanger does double duty as a Christmas tree decoration.

① Mount a photograph (we used one from a holiday vacation) on a slightly larger piece of card stock. Round all corners with a punch, and paint the edges with a gold foil pen.

② Adhere to a larger piece of leftover paper that has been backed with card stock.

③ Punch holes in the top, add a loop of wire, and embellish.

2

3

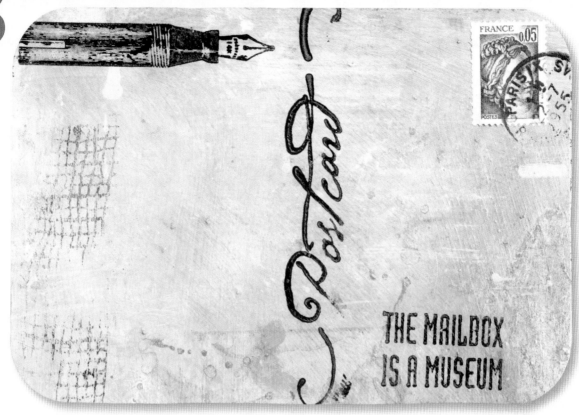

A Chance to Write "Wish You Were Here"

We will give you ten minutes to make this postcard from leftovers, and we bet you'll even have some leftover time when you are done.

① Trace the shape of an actual postcard onto the back of your leftover paper—approximately a 4" x 6" (10.2 x 15.2 cm) rectangle.

② Decorate with rubber stamps and a postage stamp.

③ Cover the back of the card with a photograph or decorative paper.

Studio Tip

If you don't have time to make leftovers right after finishing the project, keep the materials in a manila folder. Glue a strip of paper on the outside to identify the contents, and be sure to include leftovers of all the materials you used. We did this while writing this book and it helped us find exactly what we needed—a miracle indeed.

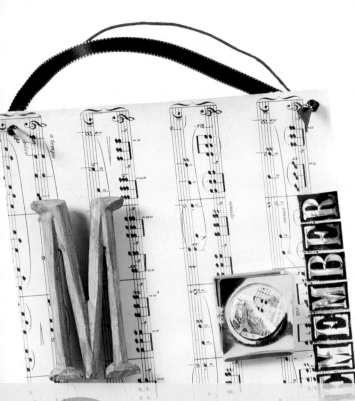

2 THE PAPER PUSHER

Making ordinary objects into *objets d'art* takes a trained eye and a dash of imagination. This intriguing collection of gifts is for folks we call paper pushers—those whose desk or work space is likely the center of their universe.

These functional pieces were designed to organize desktop items while making a statement about the person sitting in the chair. We combined household items, office supplies, an old book, a sheet of metal, and paperweights—all ordinary objects—and elevated them into stylish accessories where whimsy and function partner up.

An altered book holding clips and pushpins is "Art for Fun" at its best. Reach for one with a flower on top or attach a fashionable tab divider to your notebook. This masterpiece will make you want to reorganize the entire desktop!

Adding a name, initials, or a monogram emphasizes that the gift is made exclusively for the receiver. Photographs, a drawing, or a postcard will recall a vacation or special event, and a single word such as *art* or *write* (as seen in the collaged paperweights) conveys that you understand and honor the person's talent or passion.

Personalized gifts for the paper pusher may not affect the workload but they will certainly add personality to the work space.

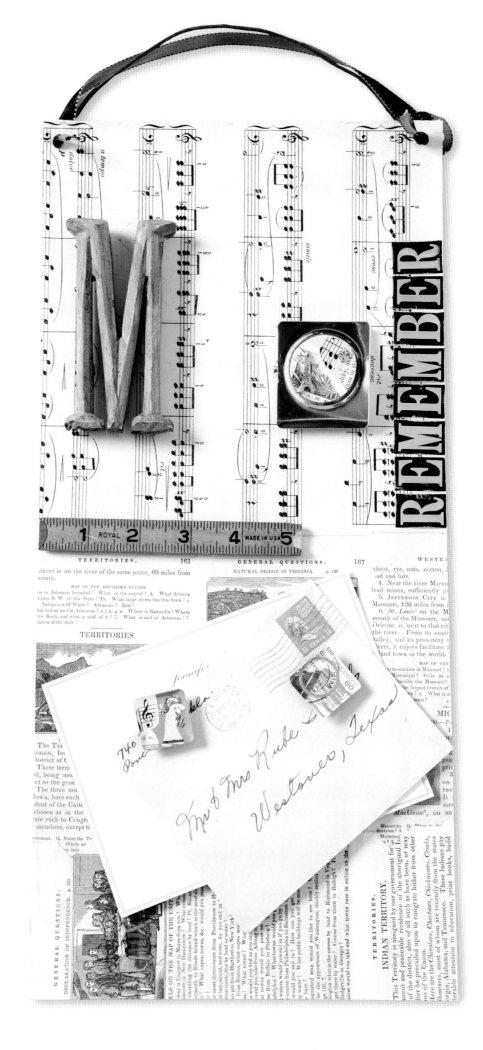

Metal Message Board

Office décor is getting hipper by the moment. Keeping track of lists, messages, and tickets is essential—and now they can look good too with this funky metal memo board. Collage materials turned into magnets help take a static message center and turn it into an interactive work of art.

MATERIALS

- metal roof flashing on a roll
- vintage papers
- decorative papers
- collage items such as mailbox stickers, wooden letters, old rulers, magnetic clips, or brass charms
- ribbons
- magnets
- clear epoxy stickers
- soft gel (gloss or matte)
- thinned acrylic paints or glazes
- glue stick
- strong, fast-drying liquid glue

TOOLS

- basic tool kit (see page 10)
- foam paintbrushes
- metal hole punch or hammer and nail

Shopping Tip

Have we mentioned how much we love going to the home improvement store? This very chic project is just one more reason to shop your local hardware or warehouse store. Look for rolls of metal flashing (used for roofs) or buy large sheets that can be custom cut for your project. Just think, you could have a whole magnetic wall in your home office!

INSTRUCTIONS

❶ Cut the metal to size using metal shears, a utility knife, and a metal-edge ruler, or a guillotine paper cutter.

❷ Spread a thin coat of the soft gel over the metal and apply the papers to create the collage. Cover the entire collage with the gel and add any thinned acrylic paints or glazes to tint or color the collage.

❸ When the board is dry, trim around the edge of the metal, punch two holes in the top of the message board, and add the ribbon for hanging.

❹ Create small collages and adhere clear epoxy stickers over them. Cut out the collages and glue them to magnets.

❺ Adhere the magnets to other movable collage items such as stained or glazed wood letters and pieces of old wood rulers. Add magnets to the message board.

COLLAGE UNDER GLASS

Paperweights

Who knew paperweights could have such personality? When you customize one of these special glass globes, you have the opportunity to create a real work of art with a special friend in mind. Look around the house for tiny knickknacks to include in these three-dimensional collages. And don't forget the velvet paper bottom—it's the final touch that completes the ultimate weighty gift.

MATERIALS

- card stock
- decorative velvet paper
- small trinkets and paper ephemera
- glue stick
- strong, fast-drying glue with a small tip opening
- paperweight

TOOLS

- basic tool kit (see page 10)

INSTRUCTIONS

1 Trace the paperweight onto the card stock base and cut it out slightly smaller so that the card stock doesn't hang over the bottom edges. Trace this onto a piece of decorative velvet paper and cut it out. Glue the velvet paper to the bottom side of the card stock to make a scratch-free base for the paperweight.

2 Add collage elements to the piece, making sure that none of the trinkets are too big to fit under the glass. Use strong liquid glue for this step and make sure to let it dry completely.

3 Run a small bead of glue around the bottom edge of the paperweight. Set it in place over the collage and let it dry completely.

Shopping Tip

Empty paperweights like these are fun to look for at flea markets, estate sales, and antique shops. We found the first two hidden in the back corner of a stamp store and then quickly found two more at a big outdoor antique show in Massachusetts for $1 each. What treasures!

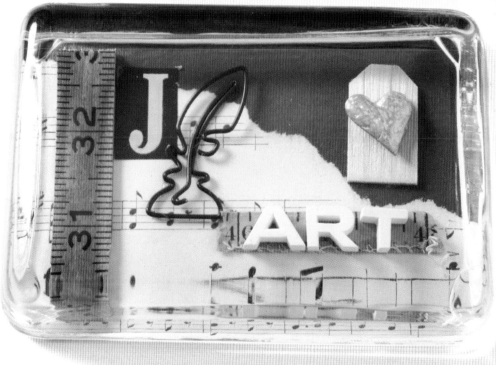

Business Card Holder

Simple and quick, this thoughtful gift holds business cards with ease and can perk up any paper pusher's day. Make the neighborhood babysitter a set of calling cards with perforated business card sheets available at the office supply store. Enclose them in a personalized business card holder and hope that she's still available to watch the little ones when the holidays roll around.

MATERIALS

- decorative papers
- eyelets
- elastic cord
- glue

TOOLS

- basic tool kit (see page 10)
- eyelet setter
- template (see page 106)

INSTRUCTIONS

1 Glue two sheets of decorative paper together back to back or use double-sided paper.

2 Trace the template onto the paper and transfer the score lines and hole placement. Cut out, score, and punch the holes.

3 Add eyelets with the right side of the eyelet on the outside of the holder, and then fold along the score lines.

4 With the inside of the holder facing you, follow the numbering guide and arrows on the template to weave the elastic cord up and down through the holder.

5 Knot the elastic cord together between holes 1 and 6. The knot will be hidden by the flap on the left side.

VARIATIONS ON A THEME

Decorative paper with polka dots makes a whimsical holder for a set of straight-laced business cards.

Tickets for a sporting event are right at home with this basketball textured paper. This masculine holder could also conceal a gift card for a favorite sporting goods store.

A **gift certificate** for a day at the spa is dressed and ready to party in swirls and checks. Or present one in this lively style to Grandma, filled with photos of the grandchildren.

Presenting **business cards** with pertinent contact information is professional business savvy. But don't succumb to a boring or traditional holder. Tell them who you are with one of these sassy carriers.

New Use for an Old Book

Hiding items between the pages of a book is a practice almost as old as books themselves. Using a book bought for a dollar, a niche is created by cutting away an opening from the center pages. While secrecy is not important here, hiding away desktop clutter is. This pocket stores all the essential things any paper pusher uses daily. But look again. Paper clips, pushpins, and binder clips have all been dressed up for way more than your typical office duties. Wrapped in old ledger paper and miniature flowers, they're ready to be useful and pretty.

MATERIALS

- vintage book
- pushpins
- corrugated cardboard
- small paper flowers and leaves
- decorative paper or paper ephemera
- card stock
- paper clips
- white shrink plastic
- plastic box
- pigment or permanent ink
- glue stick
- soft gel (matte or gloss)
- clear dimensional glaze
- binder clips

TOOLS

- basic tool kit (see page 10)
- large craft knife
- 1 1/2" (3.8 cm) circle punch
- heat gun
- stamps
- template (see page 107)

INSTRUCTIONS

To Create the Book Niche

❶ Open to the place in the book where you want the niche to begin. It is usually best to start a few pages in. Start one page behind where you want to begin. (Cut the first page after all the others have been cut for a precise fit.)

❷ Trace your plastic box onto the page, making sure to leave enough room for the hinge to open.

❸ Using a glue stick, adhere the outside edges of the book pages together. Glue only ten to fifteen pages together at a time so that it will be easier to remove the niche cutouts after you cut them.

❹ Using a metal-edge ruler and a large craft knife, start cutting around your traced line through the book, removing the center of the pages, until your niche is deep enough to hold your plastic box.

❺ Once you are done cutting through the book, finish gluing the page sets together. Using the gel, paint the inside walls of the niche. Put a piece of plastic between the niche and the front of the book to keep it from sticking, close the book, and place a weight on top until it dries.

Making Decorated Pushpins

1 Cut small strips of paper that fit around the barrel of the pins and slightly overlap.

2 Glue the strips around the pushpin barrels and wrap with a flower or leaf. You can also decorate the top of the pin with a circle of paper made from a hole punch.

Making Decorated Paper Clips

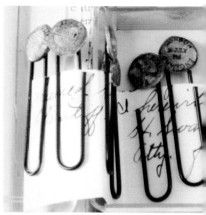

1 Rub ink over shrink plastic and stamp with an image.

2 Punch out images with the circle punch and edge with ink.

3 Shrink the pieces one at a time with a heat gun. Carefully take each piece while it is still warm and mold it over a rounded object (such as a marble) to create a domed shape.

4 Place the pieces face down, rest the end of a paper clip in each one, and fill the domed shape with clear dimensional glaze, making sure to secure the paper clip.

Making Decorated Binder Clips

1 Cut small strips of paper to fit the binder clips and glue on.

2 Embellish with small paper flowers and wind the excess stems around a thin stick to create a spiral.

Making Decorated Tabs

1 Trace tab template (see page 107) onto sturdy ledger paper and cut out.

2 Fold in half and add a small rectangle of card stock as a label.

Finish the project by inserting the plastic box into the book niche. Use cardboard, extra paper, and card stock to hold and organize the different office supplies.

Studio Tip

Creating shrink plastic–topped paper clips is a very rewarding project. Consider making a monogrammed set for a friend stamped with their initial. If you're making a number of these clips, try using the oven to shrink them all down at once and take them out one at a time to create the domed effect.

Finding Inspiration on the Road

Paper artists have been known to become downright giddy contemplating the opportunities to acquire materials for travel journals and future art projects when traveling. The obvious items are handmade papers, quality writing tools, watercolors, and blank journals. And then there are all the other possibilities: colorful lottery tickets, foil candy wrappers, and advertisements with great graphics. When you get in the right state of mind you see possibilities in most everything.

Get organized by making a list of items you might want to collect before you leave home. A recent list of mine included children's books and games, postage stamps, out-of-date playbills posted on buildings and in the metro stations, cheap items from street vendors, and food labels. Give each person you are traveling with a copy of your list and tell them to also save all the packaging materials from the stores such as sacks and wrapping papers. Many stores have stickers with their logo and are happy to throw in a few extra. In the evenings it is fun to have everyone empty their pockets and backpacks to see what they found.

Upon arrival, make your first stop the tourist information center. Sometimes they have locations both at the airport and near the town centers. Stock up on every map and brochure available. Even if you don't know exactly how you will use these items you will be glad to have them when you start putting your journal and collages together.

Many large cities have bookseller stalls along the river or in central locations. Look for old art and architecture books, pamphlets, poetry, and anything with beautiful fonts and graphics. Be sure to pick up a newspaper and a couple of glossy magazines at the newsstands. Museum stores always have artistic postcards, prints, calendars, cards, games, and puzzles.

If you are passionate about handmade and unusual papers, learn how to say paper in the language of the country you are visiting. In French it is *papier*, in Spain a paper or stationery store is called a *papeleria*, and in Italy the word for paper is *carta*.

Even if you are just a casual photographer, consider taking pictures of specific subjects such as signs with the word "art" in them, displays of produce in the open-market places, balconies, or interesting doorways. You will enjoy having a series of photographs on the same theme for more options in your artwork.

Traveling Artist Portfolio, page 20

Leftovers

Quick Ideas for Using Your Scraps

You won't need to scale down your expectations with these petite office accessories.

1

Getting a Grip

These gems are small luxuries that last and last.

① Arrange flower and leaf stickers over dictionary words.

② Place square epoxy stickers over them.

③ Cut out and glue magnets to the back. Arrange in a small tin.

Bulletin Board Bling

Almost as pretty as it is practical, this oversized pushpin does double duty holding notes, messages, and lists.

① Glue printed tissue paper to the entire plastic portion of the pushpin.

② Coat with clear acrylic when dry.

③ Twist wire around the shaft of the pushpin and coil the wire at the top. Insert cards, photos, or memorabilia between the wire coils.

2

3

Tin Pins

They say "it is all in the presentation," and this gift proves it.

① Wrap decorative paper around the stems of clear pushpins.

② Using a hole punch, punch out text dots and glue to the ends of the pushpins.

③ Cut a circle of cork and place in a round tin. Stick pins to the cork and add decorative paper to the outside of the tin.

Studio Tip

Consider making multiples for quick and easy items such as these. It does not double the time to make two instead of one when all your supplies are at hand. Since the top of the giant pushpins are large enough to hold a letter, create multiple pushpins to spell out a name, favorite word, or phrase. Who knows, perhaps big chunky numbers attached to each pushpin might even help prioritize daily to-do lists.

3 THE CHEF

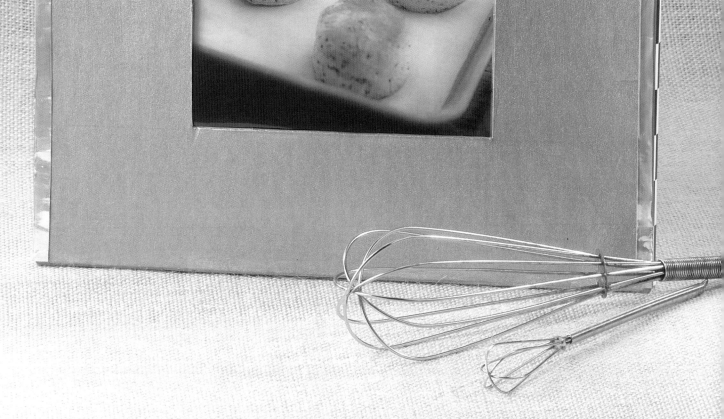

This chapter is for the host (or hostess!) who can be found in his or her element behind the stove, regaling guests with tidbits of food lore while preparing a delicious meal. It is also for those who own a wicked collection of kitchen accoutrement or shelves of cookbooks but never do anything more complex than "heat and stir." No matter what talents may be tied up in those apron strings, we celebrate them all with culinary gifts made from paper.

Recipe clipboards show up dressed and ready to party. Capable of serving many roles (yes, even rolls!) in the kitchen, they hold recipes while you cook, herald your menu from aperitif to dessert, and keep lists organized and at hand. On the counter, on the refrigerator, or on the wall, they are as welcome as a guest who comes early and offers to help.

Cookbooks may offer advice on preparing and serving artichokes, but it takes an artist to make them a feast for the eyes. We saw all those leaves as a surface for calligraphy and collage. With the addition of tiny embellishments, these decorated faux vegetables make a gift for the chef that just may upstage the meal.

Your host will appreciate our ideas for conversation starters. Give the guests something to talk about, we say! Our kitchen portfolio features a collection of food quotes on place cards. Similar to fortune cookies, everyone shares their quote or poses the question, who said this: *I come from a family where gravy is considered a beverage"?* (Erma Bombeck.)

These days the kitchen is the place to be seen—food, friends, and family is an unbeatable combination. Whether it is treasured recipes and photographs scanned onto a CD or napkin rings made from vintage cookbook pages, the projects in this chapter will help you make these occasions both personal and memorable.

Kitchen Journal

Just like an actual oven, you must first pull open the door of this kitchen portfolio to see what's cookin' inside. Behind the door you will discover a banquet of ideas for chefs and foodies who enjoy sharing their cooking while putting a personal touch on everything from paper napkin rings to copies of their signature recipes. And, since so much of family life centers around the kitchen, the portfolio can also be used as a book to gather your entertaining notes, treasured recipes, and *tasteful* photographs.

MATERIALS

- chipboard or sturdy trifold portfolio
- black file folders
- 4" x 6" (10.2 x 15.2 cm) blank recipe cards (use purchased blank recipe cards or make them from card stock)
- acetate transparency
- black chalkboard paint
- metal drawer handle and knobs
- handwritten recipes
- photographs of food
- decorative papers
- pages from old cookbooks

- gesso
- iridescent stainless steel acrylic (Golden)
- double-stick tape
- clip art

optional:

- CD and jewel case
- hook and loop fastener
- contact paper

TOOLS

- basic tool kit (see page 10)
- templates (see page 108–109)
- paintbrush

INSTRUCTIONS

For the Portfolio

❶ Cut a rectangle window in the front cover. The size will be determined by the size of your portfolio. Ours is approximately $3^1/2$" x $5^1/2$" (8.9 x 14 cm).

❷ Paint the cover with gesso. Apply two coats of stainless steel acrylic paint or spray the surface with silver paint. Cover all other outside surfaces with contact paper.

❸ Paint the inside surfaces with black chalkboard paint or acrylic paint.

❹ Print a food image onto an acetate transparency and size to fit the oven window. Affix on the inside of the window with double-stick tape.

❺ Affix the metal handle and knobs to the front of the cover.

❻ Customize the file folders to fit inside.

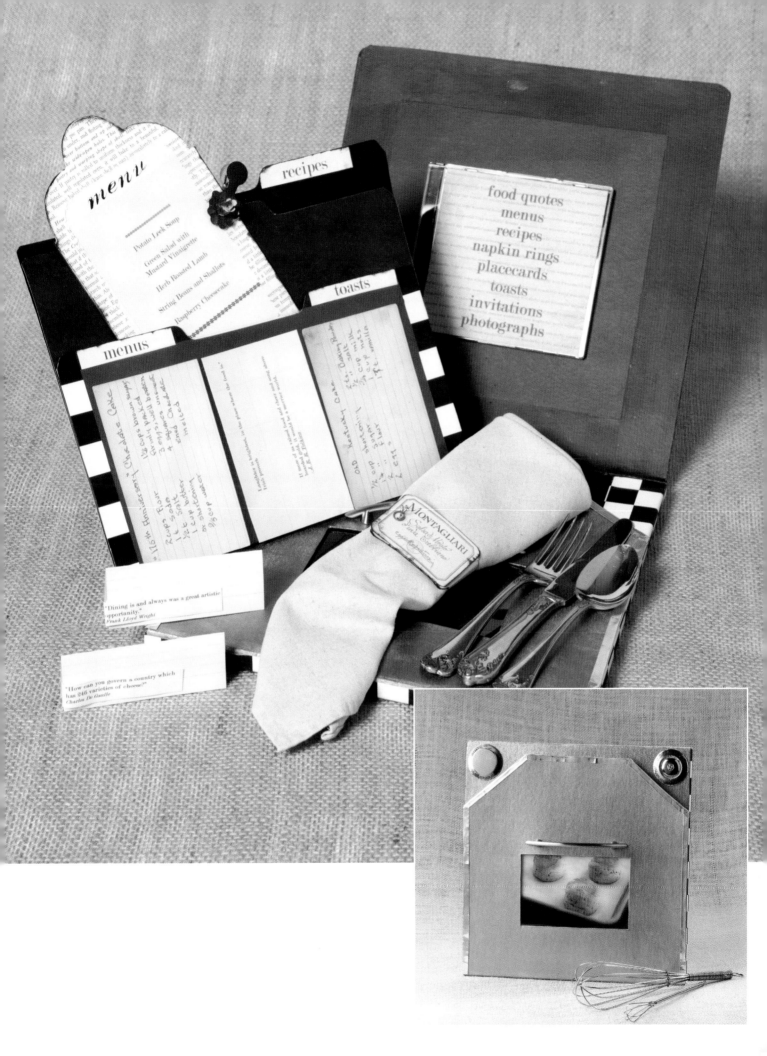

For the Menu (see a, below)

❶ Copy the menu card template on page 109 onto heavy card stock. Cut it out.

❷ Print your menu on an acetate transparency, cut to size, and attach to the front of the menu card.

For the Napkin Rings (see b, below)

❶ Copy the napkin ring template on page 108 and trace it onto decorative paper or text from an old cookbook. Cut out and bend around a napkin ring, securing the ends with the precut slits.

For the Place Cards (see page 45)

❶ Print the food quotes on page 47.

❷ Cut decorative paper or card stock measuring 4" x 3" (10.2 x 7.6 cm). Score in the center horizontally and fold, creating a "tent" card.

❸ Cut out one of the quotes and affix it to the front of the card. Add the name of a guest to the card.

For the CD Holder (see c, below)

❶ Print a table of contents for the CD on decorative paper.

❷ Attach it to the inside of the portfolio with a hook and loop fastener.

a

b

c

Food Quotes

My mother was a good recreational cook, but what she basically believed about cooking was that if you worked hard and prospered, someone else would do it for you.

—Nora Ephron

That's something I've noticed about food: whenever there's a crisis if you can get people to eating normally things get better.

—Madeleine L'Engle

Eat breakfast like a king, lunch like a prince, and dinner like a pauper.

—Adelle Davis

We are indeed much more than what we eat, but what we eat can nevertheless help us to be much more than what we are.

—Adelle Davis

Tomatoes and oregano make it Italian; wine and tarragon make it French. Sour cream makes it Russian; lemon and cinnamon make it Greek. Soy sauce makes it Chinese; garlic makes it good.

—Alice May Brock

Tell me what you eat, and I will tell you what you are.

—Calvin Trillin

The most remarkable thing about my mother is that for thirty years she served the family nothing but leftovers. The original meal has never been found.

—Calvin Trillin

Food is an important part of a balanced diet.

—Fran Lebowitz

Music with dinner is an insult both to the cook and the violinist.

—G. K. Chesterton

Good food ends with good talk.

—Geoffrey Neighor

There is no love sincerer than the love of food.

—George Bernard Shaw

Food is our common ground, a universal experience.

—James Beard

You don't have to cook fancy or complicated masterpieces—just good food from fresh ingredients.

—Julia Child

Sharing food with another human being is an intimate act that should not be indulged in lightly.

—M. F. K. Fisher

Part of the secret of success in life is to eat what you like and let the food fight it out inside.

—Mark Twain

Everything you see, I owe to spaghetti.

—Sophia Loren

A large black number sitting on the top half of the page somewhere? Who knows…

—John Keats

There is no such thing as a pretty good omelette.

—French proverb

Studio Tip

Whether your kitchen collection is for a friend or yourself, personalize it! Here are some ideas.

- Combine your own images with the templates and clip art on pages 108–109 and 118–119.
- Make the cover look like a cupboard and use an ornate teaspoon for a handle.
- Photocopy an embroidered tea towel to use on the cover.
- Enlarge copies of handwritten recipes to decorate the portfolio.
- Select a theme: the style of a specific era such as a 1950s diner, a Tuscan farmhouse, or a combination as we did: contemporary, retro, and vintage.
- Focus on the chef's specialty: grilling, baking, ethnic cuisine, and so on.
- Make the kitchen collection into a memory album with photographs and recipes from generations of family members.

ARTY-CHOKES

Kitschy Culinary Art

Sometimes it's just plain fun to create something purely decorative. These arty-chokes fall under that category. They don't hold anything, organize anything, and they certainly aren't edible. They are fun to look to at, especially when used in a centerpiece combined with actual artichokes and other fresh produce. Of course, if artichokes aren't to your taste, "art up" some eggplants or bananas.

MATERIALS

- faux artichokes
- printed tissue paper
- printed ephemera such as sheet music or maps
- small embellishments such as brass charms, game pieces, and ribbon scraps
- small letter stickers or letter die cuts
- glitter
- permanent markers
- fast-drying liquid glue
- glue stick
- permanent inks
- small rubber stamps

TOOLS

- basic tool kit (see page 10)
- awl
- decorative punches

There are no specific steps for these artichokes. Instead it's fun to just choose random leaves and alter them a bit. The instructions below detail a few ways these arty-chokes have been manipulated. You're sure to discover your own clever ideas.

INSTRUCTIONS

1 Tear small pieces of tissue or paper ephemera and layer them onto the leaves using a glue stick on the back of the paper. Use a thin instrument such as an awl to gently push the paper down between the leaves.

2 Use a permanent marker to write "artichoke" over and over on a leaf. Don't worry about your penmanship; the messier it is, the more it looks like an abstract pattern.

3 Stamp small images on random leaves with the permanent ink.

4 Poke holes through a leaf with an awl and tie on small brass charms.

5 Cut a small door in one of the leaves and tuck a small stamped game piece behind it.

6 Glue on other small embellishments.

7 Add letter stickers or small die cuts punched out of paper ephemera.

Stylish Clipboards

When the flour is flying and the sausages are sizzling, any gourmet knows it's hard to keep track of everything in the kitchen. These saucy clipboards are a perfect gift and offer just the right amount of organization without taking up too much counter space. Slide the recipe card under the clip and the chef is off and cooking. Or use one for announcing the evening's dinner menu written on heavy card stock that's been painted with chalkboard paint. Any cook would love to have one of these clipboards hanging around the kitchen. They're even good for grocery lists.

MATERIALS

- small clipboards
- decorative papers
- ribbon
- library pocket
- vintage recipe
- piece of chalk
- waxed twine
- brads
- black chalkboard paint
- heavy card stock or cardboard
- kitchen drawer knobs and washers
- bolts and wing nuts measuring 3" (7.6 cm)
- heat shrink tubing
- rubber stamps
- ink pads

optional:
- label sticker
- rub-on letters
- decoupage medium
- medallions

TOOLS

- basic tool kit (see page 10)
- drill
- heat gun
- paintbrush

INSTRUCTIONS

1. Determine and drill holes for long bolts that will create the stand for your clipboards. Alternatively, you can drill holes at the top and thread with string or a ribbon for hanging.

2. Decoupage the clipboard with decorative papers. Paint cardboard or heavy card stock with black chalkboard paint and trim to fit the clipboard.

3. Add brads, medallions, ribbon, and other embellishments.

4. Screw long bolts and wing nuts or kitchen knobs with washers to each clipboard to create a stand. Cover each bolt with heat shrink tubing and shrink with a heat gun. This will prevent the hardware from scratching kitchen surfaces.

(continued on page 52)

(continued from page 50)

5 Tie a piece of chalk to the clipboard with waxed twine.

6 Wrap a vintage recipe around a library pocket. Stamp as desired and tuck in recipes. Glue to the back of the clipboard.

Studio Tip

Clipboards come in all sizes. Experiment with sizes that will work for the cooks you know. The large kitchen knobs also make a great platform for holding a cookbook open.

FROM THE STUDIO

Finding Great Stash

In the world of mixed-media art, sources for materials are always a hot topic. Virtual and local art groups enthusiastically share information about manufacturers, websites, books, stores, and flea markets. Here's how to maximize your shopping trips:

- Research paper stores in cities or neighborhoods in which you will be shopping.

- Narrow down the list of items you are looking for, such as small boxes, marbled papers, or copper desk accessories.

- Look for potential color combinations in displays and store windows.

- Get a sense of current design trends when visiting cutting-edge boutiques.

- Be open to fresh ways to approach a project, particularly by adding or using an unexpected or unusual element, such as something found in an antique shop or at a flea market.

Remember that serendipity often plays a role in this process of discovery and acquisition.

Although you may have specific book projects in mind as you organize your hunting and gathering expeditions, you may come across something that will spur an idea that takes you in a completely different direction. Be open to these moments of inspiration, and then hurry home and start creating! Be sure to consult the extensive resources (page 120–123) that we have compiled for you before starting your next project.

Leftovers

Quick Ideas for Using Your Scraps

1

Can I Quote You on That?

Pass this library card pocket filled with food quotes from famous people around the dinner table. Each person draws one and reads it in turn—much like reading your fortune only without the cookie!

① Decorate the front of a library card pocket or envelope with a strip of text from a recipe book and a label marked "food quotes."

② Enter the words "food quotes" into a search engine and print the quotes of your choice, or find a list on page 47.

③ Cut the quotes into individual strips and place in the card pocket.

All Bottled Up

Culinary gifts deserve a tasteful presentation. With a detailed tag and wrap-around label, this glass bottle looks like it came straight from the gourmet store.

① Make a label from a strip of decorative paper. Scallop the edges using decorative scissors. Highlight with a colored marker.

② Wrap the paper around the bottle and affix with double-stick tape.

③ Thread wire through the hole on a tag and wrap securely around the neck of the bottle.

2

Recipe Trivia Book

Recipe cards double as book covers in this project, which takes about as much time to make as cooking a microwave dinner.

① Paint two 4" x 6" (10.2 x 15.2 cm) recipe cards with black paint.

② Attach together with a spine made of contact paper.

③ Adhere decorative paper on the inside surfaces and fill with food-related ephemera. Ours includes that recipe for baked possum you have been looking for.

Shopping Tip

Etiquette books and cookbooks from the 1930s and 1940s are full of social advice, recipes, and general information that is "of another era," amusing and, at times, hilarious. For instance, we found a recipe for cooking possum and advice on how to furnish the maid's alcove in an apartment. We see these gems of wisdom printed on napkin rings, tucked into place cards, or used as a way to get any gathering off to a lively start. (Although you should be aware of copyright laws in your use of vintage books, anything goes in the confines of your home!)

4 THE GIRLFRIEND

What could possibly be a better greeting than, "Hey girlfriend!"? We vote for this one: "Hey girlfriend, *I made you a gift!*" That is because a girlfriend *gets you*: she knows your signature color is spring green, that you hate (or love) mid-century modern, and that you treasure anything handmade—especially paper art. And hey you: "Girlfriend-Reading-this-Book." Better go get a new pair of socks before you proceed any further because these gift ideas are going to knock yours off.

First, let's talk, ahem … about how *unorganized* your girlfriend is. The Button Book (we don't call it a best seller for nothing) will actually ensure that when she wears her cashmere cardigan it will have all the buttons—and they will all match! The book has compartments for clothing tags, care instruction labels, pins, needles, and thread. Oh, we know what you're thinking. Be assured, this is not your grandma's sewing kit.

For girlfriends who didn't make it to the Paris flea market this year, we have French Flower Buckets and the flowers to go in them. For the literary jewelry divas, check out the Journal Necklace. And let's not forget the Origami Writing Set—a stylish thank-you note for acknowledging those artful gifts.

Origami Writing Set

Penning a letter will never go out of style. And no matter how many emails we send or teleconferences we have, the handwritten note remains sacred. It's the perfect way to say "thank you" to your weekend hostess. Or, "it was a pleasure meeting you," after an interview. In both business and our personal lives, a letter can say everything about you. And so can the stationery.

This convenient portfolio holds elegant note cards and envelopes for the woman who wants to make an impact. Understated bows mark the front of each card and a coordinating envelope completes the collection. Plaid ribbon not only adds texture but keeps the folder closed and its contents in place.

MATERIALS

- two-sided decorative paper 18" x 18" (45.7 x 45.7 cm)
- coordinating light and dark decorative paper
- envelopes
- card stock
- 38" (96.5 cm) length of sheer ribbon
- glue stick
- foam adhesive

TOOLS

- basic tool kit (see page 10)

INSTRUCTIONS

Making the Origami Holder

1 Choose the side of the paper to be the primary color on the outside. Fold the paper in half with the primary color on the outside and crease with a bone folder. Open the paper back up.

2 With the primary color facing up and the center fold vertical, fold the right-hand edge in to meet the center fold. This makes a quarter fold. Open back out (see **a**).

3 Fold the right panel in half again by aligning the left edge with the quarter fold. These are the secondary color panels. Do not open back out (**b**).

4 Repeat steps 2 and 3 on the left side.

5 On the bottom of the right secondary panel, fold a triangle by bringing the bottom horizontal edge to meet the right side. Repeat on the bottom left corner.

(continued on page 60)

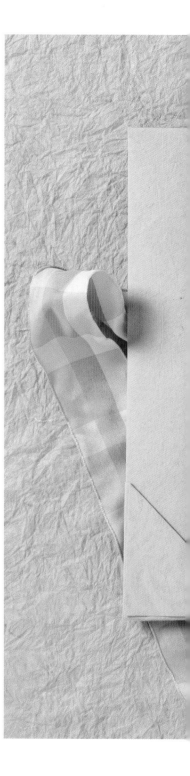

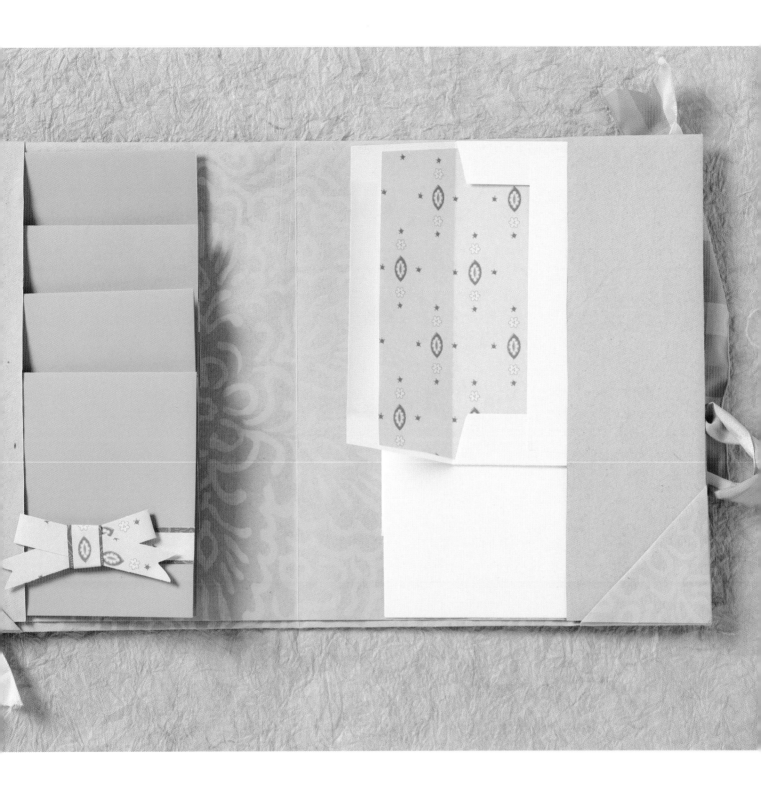

(continued from page 58)

6 Along the bottom edge, fold under a 2 1/4" (5.7 cm) panel (which should align with the triangle).

7 Turn the paper over so that the secondary color is facing up and the 2 1/4" (5.7 cm) panel is along the bottom (**c**).

8 Take the top edge of the paper and fold it down until it meets the bottom edge, and tuck the right and left corners under the triangle folds to secure (**d**).

9 Thread the sheer ribbon through these panels. Tie the portfolio closed (**e**).

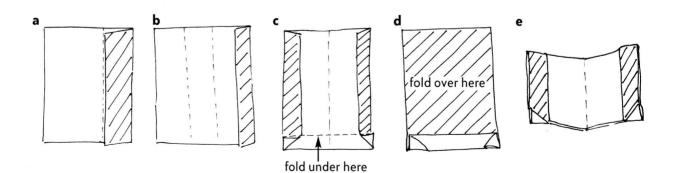

a   b   c   fold under here   d   fold over here   e

Making the Stationery

1 Cut card stock to 5$\frac{1}{2}$" x 8$\frac{1}{2}$" (14 x 21.6 cm) and fold in half to make the cards.

2 Cut eight strips of light decorative paper $\frac{1}{2}$" x 4$\frac{1}{2}$" (1.3 x 11.4 cm).

3 Cut a dovetail (V-shaped) finish on one end of each strip.

4 Make a fold 1$\frac{1}{2}$" (3.8 cm) from the other end of each strip and fold under creating one bow loop.

5 Cut three strips of light decorative paper $\frac{1}{2}$" x 12" (1.3 x 30.5 cm). Cut three strips of dark decorative paper $\frac{5}{8}$" x 12" (1.6 x 30.5 cm). Glue the light strips in the center of the dark strips.

6 From these strips cut four strips 5$\frac{1}{2}$" (14 cm) long and four strips 1$\frac{3}{4}$" (4.4 cm) long.

7 Glue one of the 5$\frac{1}{2}$" (14 cm) strips across each card front 1" (2.5 cm) from the bottom edge of the card.

8 Cross two bow loops to create a bow and wrap one of the 1$\frac{3}{4}$" (4.4 cm) strips of paper around the bow. Secure with glue and adhere to the card with a foam adhesive.

Beautiful on the Inside: Lining an Envelope

Lining the envelopes for this project takes only a moment and makes an ordinary envelope extraordinary in just seconds. In coordinating a note card with an envelope you add a hint of letter-writing tradition with a fresh, modern appeal. Regardless of the envelope shape the procedure is the same.

1 On the back of a piece of decorative paper trace an envelope with the flap open.

2 Cut this shape out of the decorative paper, making sure to cut the top about $\frac{1}{2}$" (1.3 cm) shorter and the sides $\frac{1}{8}$" (3 mm) shorter on each side.

3 Slip this decorative paper into the envelope so that the adhesive along the envelope edge is still visible and is evenly aligned on each side.

4 Lift up the top flap of the liner and use a glue stick around the top of this flap. It is not necessary to put glue on the entire liner because the top will hold everything in place.

5 Fold the envelope flap back down, using a bone folder to reinforce the crease.

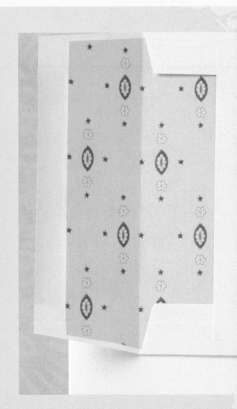

French Flower Buckets

Reminiscent of a French flower market, our faux tin paper buckets are billowing with multicolored paper flowers. They would be a gift appreciated by everyone from girlfriends and hostesses to mothers-in-law and neighbors. When the flowers fade, the buckets can be used to hold art supplies, cards and letters, and favorite catalogs.

Techniques to make the paper buckets look like tin or faded paint are easier than you may think. And when you add one of the French labels from the clip art section on page 118 to your finished bucket, you will see how quickly a piece of poster board and a little paint can become a useful and lovely *objet d'art* with many uses.

MATERIALS

- white poster board
- vintage label (see page 118)
- acrylic paint: silver, light gray, dark gray, black
- gesso
- double-stick tape
- clear adhesive dots (Therm O Web Zots)
- wire for the handle

optional:

- silver spray paint
- silver foil pen
- paper towels

TOOLS

- basic tool kit (see page 10)
- paintbrush
- clip art (see page 118)

INSTRUCTIONS

Bucket Construction

❶ Lay out the measurements for the bucket on poster board: 22" (55.9 cm) across the top, 14$\frac{1}{2}$" (36.8 cm) across the bottom, connected by 13" (33 cm) lines for the sides. Cut.

❷ Decorate the poster board as desired (see Painting Faux Tin instructions below).

❸ Place a line of glue dots down one side of the poster board. Bend the other side around and affix it to the glue dots.

❹ Fold up a $\frac{3}{4}$" (1.9 cm) hem on the bottom of the bucket and affix it to the backside with glue dots.

❺ Punch a hole on each side to hold the wire handle.

❻ Cut a piece of wire approximately 18" (45.7 cm) and bend it into the shape of a handle.

❼ Insert the ends of the wire through the holes and bend them to secure.

Painting Faux Tin

1 Use a straight-edge ruler and a bone folder to make horizontal lines across the back of the poster board.

2 Pour about two tablespoons each of silver, light gray, and dark gray acrylic paint onto a paper plate.

3 Pick up some of each of the three colors on a 2" (5.1 cm) brush and apply to the front of the poster board in horizontal strokes.

4 When the surface is covered in the various shades of gray, stipple areas of the surface with the silver and dark gray paint.

5 Using a dry brush, apply white gesso sparingly in a random pattern for an aged effect.

6 Using a straight-edge ruler, apply a thin line of black paint under each of the horizontal lines created with the bone folder. While the paint is wet, dab the poster board with a paper towel to lighten some areas.

7 Paint a $^1/_4$" (6 mm) line around the top of the bucket with dark gray paint.

8 If desired, use a silver foil pen to apply a thin line beneath the black lines to add depth. Adhere vintage labels.

QUICK PAINTING METHOD: After cutting out the poster board, spray the board with silver paint. Let dry and continue from instruction 3 in the preceding bucket construction instructions.

Les Nouvelles **Plantes & Fleurs** D'APPARTEMENT

VARIATIONS ON A THEME

Matte-finish paint and gesso result in a vintage painted look for a bucket. A French clip art label completes the look.

Edible gifts can be left on the neighbor's door in this anaglyphic pocket. Cut from a roll of wallpaper and made pretty with a ribbon handle, this miniature version is quick to make.

Hearts and flowers unite on this bucket fashioned from scrapbook papers. Touches of machine stitching and pom-pom fringe punctuate its girly personality.

Paper Flowers

The templates and illustrations for making paper flowers are merely to get you started. They are so easy you will be soon designing your own blooms by changing the shape and size of the leaves and petals and by adding sparkle and glitter. We upped Mother Nature with our two-sided leaves made from designs she never envisioned, and we bet six peonies that you will too.

MATERIALS

- solid color papers
- decorative papers
- crepe paper
- green florist wire
- green florist tape
- spray glue or paper glue
- glue dots
- gold foil pen

TOOLS

- basic tool kit (see page 10)
- wire cutters
- 2" (5.1 cm) paintbrush or foam brush
- decorative-edge scissors
- templates (see page 110)

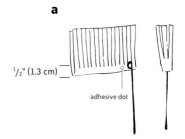

a

½" (1.3 cm) ⎯

adhesive dot

INSTRUCTIONS

Pink Wired Flower

1 Make the center of the flower by cutting a strip of paper measuring 5" x 5$^1/_2$" (12.7 x 14 cm). Fold in half horizontally. On the unfolded edge, make 1$^1/_2$" (3.8 cm)-long cuts at approximately $^1/_8$" (3 mm) intervals. Leave a $^1/_2$" (1.3 cm) uncut border at the bottom of the strip (see **a**).

2 Make a small loop at the top of a length of florist wire. Apply a glue dot to the side of the paper fringe and wind tightly around the loop. Secure with a glue dot (**a**).

3 To make the petals, trace the petal template (see page 108) and cut ten petals.

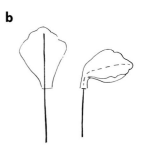

b

4 Place a piece of wire measuring 6" (15.2 cm) along the center length of the petal, apply glue, and place another petal on top. Let dry (**b**).

5 Hold the petal next to the fringed flower center, wrapping the base of the petal to the wire stem with florist tape (**c**). Attach the remaining petals.

c

6 Make and attach the leaves to the stems in the same fashion.

Purple Ruffled Flower

❶ Make the flower center and attach to the stem as instructed in the Pink Wired Flower. For a variation, use decorative scalloped scissors for the top edge and make a $1/4$" (6 mm) vertical cut between each scallop (see **a**).

❷ Cut out five petals using the template on page 110.

❸ Attach another piece of wire to the stem wire as shown in the diagram (**b**).

❹ Fold the petal in half and gather it onto the wire. Repeat with the remaining petals (**b**).

❺ Wind the wire tightly around the stem, evenly spacing the petals as you go (**c**).

❻ Wrap with florist tape and add leaves as described above for the Pink Wired Flower (**d**).

a   **b**   **c**   **d**

Variation for Flower Center

❶ For the center of the flower, roll a small ball (about the size of a marble) of tissue paper. Make a loop on the end of a piece of wire and insert the loop into the center of the ball. Cover the ball with a piece of colored tissue and secure it at the bottom with a 2" (5.1 cm) piece of wire wound tightly at the base of the tissue ball.

❷ See step 1 of the Pink Wired Flower instructions (see page 68) for adding paper fringe. Apply a glue dot to the side of the paper fringe and wind tightly around the base of the tissue-covered ball. This center can be used with either the wired or the gathered petals.

Journal Necklace

With a nod to the sentimental tradition of wearing jewelry that holds a photo of a loved one, this updated version of a locket is redesigned and full of surprises. This version is a tiny accordion journal that folds neatly into a metal picture frame.

Decorating both sides of the accordion provides ample space for you to combine photographs, text, and artwork. The result is a playful juxtaposition of collage and memory art. And, with varied and unusual embellishments—from torn paper hearts to itsy-bitsy rickrack downsized to match the proportion of the tiny book—the finished piece is whimsical and…dare we say precious?

Themes for this gift might be based on your friendship and times spent together or commemorate a milestone event, a vacation, or motherhood. Whether this recipient is an animal lover, an avid reader, a musician, athlete, gardener, or writer, this mini-masterpiece can be personalized to honor you friend's unique talents and passions.

MATERIALS

- brass locket
- decorative paper
- small photographs
- permanent ink
- embellishments such as rub-on letters, old postage stamps, or rhinestone stickers
- beads
- jump rings
- cotton or leather cord
- two jewelry crimp ends to fit the cord
- lobster clasp
- rubber stamps

TOOLS

- basic tool kit (see page 10)
- needle-nose pliers
- decorative-edge scissors

INSTRUCTIONS

Making the Necklace

1 Stamp a subtle pattern with permanent ink on the brass locket. Add a jump ring to the top.

2 Cut the cotton or leather cord to the desired length. Thread the cord through the jump ring and add a bead to both sides of the jump ring. Center the locket and beads, then tie an overhand knot in the cord next to each bead to hold everything in place.

3 Trim the ends of the cord if necessary to make them even. Add crimp ends by inserting the cord and squeezing the sides closed with pliers.

4 Add jump rings to both crimp ends and add a lobster clasp to one of the jump rings.

Making the Booklet Insert

1 Cut a piece of sturdy decorative paper to $1^{1}/_{2}$" x $8^{3}/_{8}$" (3.8 x 21.3 cm). Fold this strip into eight even panels to create an accordion-folded booklet.

2 Close the booklet and orient it so that the first page opens like a book. This first page is the cover. Decorate it with embellishments as desired.

3 Open the rest of the book so that you can see all the panels (the cover will be facing your work surface now).

4 Decorate with embellishments and photographs. Use decorative-edge scissors to cut mats for the photos as desired. Finish decorating the reverse side.

5 Fold the booklet back up and insert it into the locket.

Shopping Inspirations

The Mixed Mediums are advocates of getting out and about. Call it shopping if you must, but this shared experience is vital to our art and writing books. Our shopping jaunts rarely have a specific purpose. Instead, it's about being out together and seeing things that lead to uncharted territory—maybe a bit like the Lewis and Clark expedition.

During one of our intense meetings while planning the book we had to escape to the outside world for some fresh air, inspiration… and food. We headed to San Juan Capistrano in southern California. This mission town is steeped in history and has a good sampling of the kinds of the unusual stores we seek. We struck gold at our first stop.

The sounds of splashing water lured us into the courtyard where we navigated a maze of architectural pieces for home and garden. We sighed over curvaceous wrought iron gates, glazed planters, and old signs. It was at the moment when we spotted some very funky folded metal pockets sporting French documents that we knew we'd found something significant. We all started talking at once about the possibilities. It met our criteria for something we would want in our home and that was an unusual example of decorative art that could be made from paper.

We hurried back to the studio with visions of materials to experiment with: anaglyphic wallpaper, decorative paper accented with sewn edges, and faux painting techniques to mimic tin and wood. This well-spent afternoon resulted in the French Flower Buckets project on page 62.

The Button Book

Giving the gift of organization may seem like a boring or tedious idea, but when that gift comes on a giant metal ring with a ribbon you will be tempted to get out granny's old button tin! Sandwiched between the pages of this easily constructed swing book are the supplies to keep and sew buttons (and darn a few socks). Use a stapler to add packets of extra buttons that come with new garments. Keep the permanent pen handy to make additional labels to identify the buttons for later use. And if that isn't enough, the unique embroidery using small paper strips in place of thin ribbon adds to the charm of this one-of-a-kind organizer.

MATERIALS

- buttons
- decorative card stock
- thin cardboard
- ribbon
- small ribbon buckle
- brads
- rickrack
- die-cut alphabet letters
- permanent pen
- glassine envelope
- sticker sheet
- stapler (to use as a dangling tool on the spine)
- felt scrap

- small sewing kit with thread spools, needles, pins, and scissors
- metal ring
- small plastic bags
- glue stick
- foam adhesive
- fast-drying liquid glue

TOOLS

- basic tool kit (see page 10)
- templates (see page 109)
- clip art (see page 118)
- decorative-edge scissors
- $1/8$" and $1/4$" (3 and 6 mm) hole punches
- round corner punch

INSTRUCTIONS

Making the Pages

1 Cut out ten (or more) pieces of thin cardboard 4" x 6" (10.2 x 15.2 cm). Use the glue stick to adhere the decorative card stock to the cardboard. Trim around the edges to even up the sides.

2 Use decorative-edge scissors to cut the right edge of each page and round the two left-hand corners with the corner rounder.

3 Punch a $1/4$" (6 mm) hole in the left side of each cardboard page (refer to the template on page 109 for placement).

Making the First Page

1 Punch a $1/8$" (3 mm) hole about $1/4$" (6 mm) from the top of the first page and tie a permanent pen to the page with a ribbon.

2 Cut the sticker paper into $5/8$" x 2" (1.6 x 5.1 cm) strips. Use the $1/4$" (6 mm) hole punch to round the corners as shown in the photograph.

3 Put the stickers into a small glassine envelope, adhere it to the page, and attach a label.

Making the Button Pages

Leave a number of pages blank, and on the other pages staple plastic bags filled with spare buttons divided by color.

Making the Sewing Kit

1 Punch two small holes on the left side of the page (as seen in the photograph) and attach the scissors with a piece of ribbon.

2 Cut a $1^3/4$" x $3^1/2$" (4.4 x 8.9 cm) piece of felt and adhere this to the middle of the page with the liquid glue. Add pins and needles.

3 Cut a small piece of scrap cardboard $1^1/4$" x $3^1/2$" (3.1 x 8.9 cm) and cover it with the same size piece of decorative paper.

Making the Cover

1 Cut and cover a 3" x 4" (7.6 x 10.2 cm) piece of cardboard with decorative paper.

2 Add die cut letters and buttons. Punch $1/4$" (6 mm) holes referring to the template for placement.

3 Cut $1/4$" x 9" (0.6 x 22.9 cm) strips of decorative card stock for the embroidery. Crumple up the strips and roll them into small balls to loosen the fibers. Follow the illustrations to make daisy-chain stitches, shown right. Follow the template on page 109 to complete the embroidery.

4 Use foam adhesive to attach this piece to the cover and decorate with buttons.

Making a Daisy Chain Stitch

Thread all the pages on the metal ring, and add the stapler with ribbon and a bow.

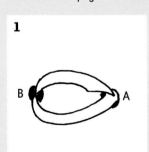

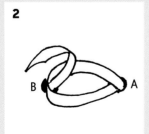

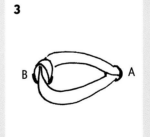

1. Bring the paper up through hole A and back down into hole A, leaving a loop that reaches to hole B.

2. Bring the paper up through hole B and into the first loop.

3. Thread the paper over the loop to secure it and thread it back into hole B.

4. Make a knot in a piece of paper ribbon and thread both ends into the center hole.

Leftovers
Quick Ideas for Using Your Scraps

Blue Ribbon Winner

In this supreme makeover, a generic metal clip is transformed into a festive and functional accessory to display cards or photos.

① Decoupage the base of a binder clip with scraps of decorative papers and old postage.

② Tie scraps of ribbon around the metal pinchers of the clip.

③ Slip a photo or business card into the top of the holder.

An Enveloping Idea

You will think of at least ten ways to use this quick and versatile template. Sweet treats or a sachet are two ideas to get you started.

① Glue squares of anaglyphic paper and decorative paper back to back, and lay the square down with the decorative paper facing up.

② With one corner pointing towards you, fold the two side corners to meet in the center. Fold the bottom corner up to meet and secure with glue or tape.

③ Add eyelets to both sides of the envelope and attach a wire handle.

3

M Is for Monogram

Everyone you know will thank you for a set of these, and your children can be enlisted to turn them out by the dozens.

① Fold black card stock into 1^1/2" (3.8 cm) squares.

② Glue die-cut letters to the front corner of each card.

③ Punch a hole at the fold and thread with ribbon and a bead.

Shopping Tip

Many products are available to add words, phrases, names, and initials to your projects. Stickers, rub-ons, stamps, and die-cut letters expand your design possibilities. Alphabet letters in chipboard, wood, plastic, fabric, and other materials make it possible to turn an average project into something to write home about.

5 THE GIVER

Who is "The Giver"? It's anyone who loves to create gifts, wrap them in gorgeous packaging, and polish them off with just the right card. Momma wasn't wrong when she said, "presentation is everything."

This chapter is about the "ta-da" factor: that all-important presentation. Get ready for festive, clever, simple, and downright gorgeous ideas for embellishing packages and designing cards. And, the best part is that everything is made from paper.

Our Gift Tag Folios organize small tags ready to add a bit of instant glamour to any gift. Tie one around a bottle of olive oil. Fantastico—an elegant hostess gift! Tags are less formal than cards; it makes sense to keep an ample supply on hand in many colors, shapes, and styles. And, a collection of decorated tags held together on a chain or metal ring is not only enjoyable to make…it makes a useful gift.

Need a quick wrap? Try a Gift Bag Pennant. Nothing says "gift" like a colorful purchased bag flying a sassy pennant secured onto a dowel. No need for a card with this gift; the packaging says it all.

Looking for a bit more elegance? Try our bonbon-type box constructed using CD pockets. Imagine it filled with truffles wrapped in foil. And while those CD pockets featured in the Supreme Makeover project are handy, they're great for a quick card. Just slip in an image, picture, or greeting, and slap it onto folded card stock and you are out the door.

And what says *party* better than a garland? Choose from two different styles: garland cards, strung together with witty greetings, can be given instead of a traditional card, or dress up boxes with paper garlands. Reminiscent of accordion-style paper dolls, these perky bows ring boxes with irresistible girly style. Lack of time is no longer an excuse for not making cards: The Big Easy teaches you how to make them in minutes with the help of paper punches and stickers.

Composition-Book Cards

Packed with so many good things to love, these cards are constructed using mini-composition booklets. Look for them during your back-to-school shopping. They can be picked up for a song! The pocket you create in the back from a coin envelope can hold a personal note, or tuck in concert tickets, a gift certificate, or a favorite recipe. The thought and detail behind one of these cards is evident upon first look.

MATERIALS

- decorative paper
- card stock
- small composition book
- coin envelope
- ribbon
- watercolor paper
- stamps or other ephemera
- decorative paper clips
- glue stick
- colored markers

TOOLS

- basic tool kit (see page 10)
- corner rounder

INSTRUCTIONS

1 Use a craft knife to carefully cut the string holding the paper in the composition book. Remove the paper.

2 Use a marker to color the outside edges of the book cover.

3 Cover the outside and inside of the cover with the decorative paper using a glue stick. Trim the edges of the cover with a craft knife if necessary.

4 Cut the watercolor paper into one (or more) inside pages measuring 4" x 6" (10.2 x 15.2 cm) by tearing it with the metal-edge ruler.

(continued on page 85)

(continued from page 82)

5 Fold the page in half and insert it into the cover.

6 Punch three holes in the spine of the cover and inside pages; place the holes 1" (2.5 cm) from the top and bottom and one in the center.

7 Lace the ribbon through the spine to attach the page(s) (see **a**).

8 Cut 2^1/2" (6.4 cm) off the bottom of the coin envelope to create a pocket. Referring to the photograph, round the top two corners and fold the front down creating a flap.

9 Cut layers of card stock, decorative paper, and watercolor paper to create an insert for the pocket as desired.

10 Embellish with stamps, ephemera, and decorative paper clips.

a

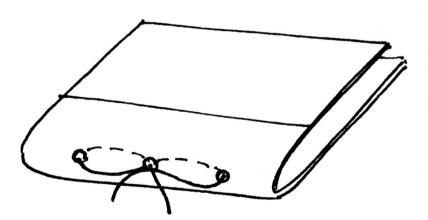

20-Minute Cards

The best part of this gift is that it's incredibly easy and quick. We've even made a set with preschoolers to give as holiday gifts for their teachers. The trick is in the supplies and setting them up in an assembly line. When the cards are all made, use the leftover scraps of matching paper and ribbon to tie them up for a gift that needs no wrapping!

MATERIALS

- card stock
- paint chips
- decorative paper
- envelopes
- three-dimensional stickers
- ribbon
- glue stick
- die-cut tags

TOOLS

- basic tool kit (see page 10)
- decorative-edge scissors
- large tag punch

INSTRUCTIONS

1 Cut card stock to $5^1/2$" x $8^1/2$" (14 x 21.6 cm) and fold in half to make a card.

2 Punch large tags out of paint chips or decorative paper.

3 Attach three-dimensional stickers to the tags.

4 Punch a hole in the tags and tie them together with a 3" (7.6 cm) piece of ribbon.

5 Glue the tags to the card front.

6 If desired, create lined envelopes (see page 61).

7 Create a wrap by layering two 12" (30.5 cm) strips of decorative paper of varying widths. (Use decorative-edge scissors if desired.)

8 Stack the envelopes and cards together.

9 Fold the 12" (30.5 cm) wrap around the stack and secure in the back with a glue stick.

10 Cut a 24" (61 cm) piece of ribbon and tie a bow around the wrap.

Shopping Tip

Many large chain stores carry blank cards and envelopes. These well-designed products are colorful, sometimes even embossed, and very trendy. Rather than starting from scratch, we suggest that you purchase these ready-made cards, then spend a few minutes customizing with your stash of embellishments. It is your personal style that makes greeting cards one-of-a-kind!

When choosing three-dimensional stickers, look for packages that have multiples of the same sticker or collections where all the stickers are approximately the same size so that it will be easy to recreate multiple cards.

Gift Tag Folios

Do you make this lovely folio for yourself or as a gift for someone else? We couldn't decide either. The tags can easily be personalized for a special gift. Consider the recipient's favorite hobby, collection, or occupation as inspiration for a special set of tags.

MATERIALS

- card stock
- decorative paper (8" x 11" [20.3 x 27.9 cm]) and scraps
- mat boards (4" x 8" [10.2 x 20.3 cm])
- eyelets
- ribbons and fibers
- elastic cord
- glue stick
- removable tape

TOOLS

- basic tool kit (see page 10)
- corner punches
- eyelet setter

INSTRUCTIONS

1 Cover the mat boards in decorative paper using a glue stick. Burnish with a bone folder to ensure good adhesion.

2 With the printed side of the paper facedown, make six score lines on the decorative paper parallel to the short side (from the left-hand side of the paper: $1^1/2$", $1^9/16$", $5^3/4$", $6^1/8$", $10^3/8$", $10^7/16$" (3.8, 4.0, 14.6, 15.6, 26.4, 26.5 cm).

3 The two center score lines will create the spine of the book. Cut a piece of decorative paper 8" x $1^1/2$" (20.3 x 3.8 cm) and glue it over this spine on the unprinted side of the paper.

4 Add two eyelets for the ribbon, one 2" (5.1 cm) from the left side and the other $1^1/4$" (3.1 cm) from the right side, both 4" (10.2 cm) from the top. Run a 24" (61 cm) piece of ribbon through these eyelets.

5 Fold the left flap $1^1/2$" (3.8 cm) in, creating the pocket that will hold the tags. Tuck one of the covered mat boards into this flap completely and hold in place temporarily with removable tape. Use eyelets to secure the flap to the board only (see photograph for placement). Do not go through the outside cover.

6 Make a small ribbon loop with 3" (7.6 cm) of ribbon and glue this under the left mat board to make a pen holder (see photograph for placement). Glue the left mat board into place.

7 Down the middle of the second mat board, evenly place eyelets at 1", $1^3/4$", $3^5/8$", $4^3/8$", $6^1/4$", and 7" (2.5, 4.4, 9.2, 11.1, 15.8, and 17.8 cm). Run a piece of elastic cord through these holes and glue the board down to the right-hand side of the folio with the $1/2$" (1.3 cm) flap on the right side wrapping around to the front.

8 Cut 2" x $3^1/2$" (5.1 x 8.9 cm) tags out of card stock and trim the corners with corner punches or decorative-edge scissors. Add decorative reinforcements to the tags. Add ribbon or fibers under the elastic holders.

VARIATIONS ON A THEME

Generic enough for anyone to use, these tags make the perfect hostess gift.

Use this version when you're short on time. This simplified adaptation was inspired by a bit of ribbon and retro-themed decorative paper.

This folio is all girl. Contrast vintage-inspired and contemporary-patterned papers with dark chocolate brown and sassy pink ribbon for a stunning project.

Use simple-patterned paper and colors when creating a folio so that it will be easy to fill and refill the tags and fibers without having to track down the original papers.

May I Have a Word? Garland

Paper garlands are a fresh and unexpected way to share a message with a friend. A spin on the traditional greeting card, this linked paper chain of words is also a decorative accessory. Hang one over a doorway, tie another one between trees in the backyard, and don't forget the mantle.

Choose a favorite sentiment or quote and spell it out using coordinating card stock and decorative papers. Making one garland takes about the same time a card does. And, you can dress them up with embellishments, pretty ribbons, and exotic papers. Once your garland is assembled you can easily place it in an envelope for mailing or make several and use them as party decorations.

Shopping Tip

Look for decorative premade tags available at scrap-booking stores. They are often sold on a 12" x 12" (30.5 x 30.5 cm) page and coordinate in several different styles. They punch out and are handy when you need a quick garland.

MATERIALS

- card stock
- eyelets
- ribbon, fibers, or twine
- rub-on letters and words
- die-cut letters

optional:

- decorative paper

- paper flowers
- rhinestones

TOOLS

- basic tool kit (see page 10)
- decorative-edge scissors
- eyelet setter

INSTRUCTIONS

❶ Decide on a phrase or sentiment for your garland.

❷ Cut out a shape from the card stock for each word.

❸ Add your message with rub-on letters, words, or die-cut letters.

❹ Punch two holes at the edges of each shape. Set eyelets in the holes as desired.

❺ String the shapes together with ribbon, fibers, or twine. Embellish as desired.

Gift Bag Pennants

Giving the wrapping of a gift as much attention as the handmade gift inside can be a challenge for any of us. Even when pressed for time, a colorful bag with a festive pennant waving from the top will earn you a cheer from your audience. Inspired by collegiate sports pennants, these can be made in all shapes and sizes, and can even use leftover materials from the handmade gift tucked inside. They are quick and easy to make with decorative-edge scissors and dowels on hand. You can customize your own or refer to pages 112–113 for templates of the ones shown here.

MATERIALS

- decorative paper
- $1/8$" (3 mm) wooden dowels
- embellishments such as rub-on letters, die cuts, stickers, tags, flowers
- ribbon
- markers

TOOLS

- basic tool kit (see page 10)
- templates (see pages 112–113)
- decorative-edge scissors

INSTRUCTIONS

Creating the Pennant

❶ Create a pennant shape or trace the template with decorative paper.

❷ Glue this shape to a second piece of paper and cut around the first shape with straight or decorative-edge scissors, leaving a small border around the initial pennant. Repeat if desired.

Decorating the Dowel

❶ Use scissors to carefully cut the dowel to size.

❷ Color the dowel with a marker, or wrap a thin strip of decorative paper around the dowel on an angle to create a stripe.

Embellishing the Pennant

❶ Use a ribbon to tie the small pennants together.

❷ Punch holes in the pennant to thread the dowel through the pennant. Wrap one end of the pennant around the dowel and glue the overlap down in the back. Tie scraps of ribbon on the dowel tops.

❸ Embellish the dowel tops with small tags or flowers.

Well-Dressed Office Supplies

MATERIALS

- one-piece purchased box measuring 4" x 6" (10.2 x 15.2 cm)
- decorative wrapping paper
- tape
- adhesive CD pockets
- decorative scrapbook papers
- card stock
- ribbon approximately $1^1/2$" (3.8 cm) wide
- twine or yarn approximately 6" (15.2 cm) long
- adhesive glue dots

TOOLS

- basic tool kit (see page 10)
- decorative-edge scissors

One of our favorite items from the office supply store is the adhesive-back CD pocket. Not to be confused with the hard plastic CD cases, these measure approximately 5" x 5" (12.7 x 12.7 cm), are made from clear, flexible plastic front, and stay put—very put. They have the "what if" factor, meaning that they challenge us to use them in both functional and decorative applications.

We dressed them up with papers, fancy-cut borders, buttons, and ribbon printed with words and phrases. For more CD pocket fun take a look at the next project.

INSTRUCTIONS

This gift resembles a giant bonbon with its dome shape and candy colors. It is amazing what a yard of gorgeous vintage ribbon can do to notch up plastic pockets!

1 Cover the box with wrapping paper and secure with tape.

2 Make a vertical slit measuring $1^3/4$" (4.4 cm) on the sides of the CD pocket near the edge, approximately $1^1/2$" (3.8 cm) from the bottom. (The length of the cut will be determined by the width of the ribbon.)

3 Make a tag from card stock to fit inside the pocket using a combination of papers. We layered a patterned paper, a small check, and a solid color.

4 Use decorative-edge scissors to cut a scalloped border on each tag.

5 Make a paper loop $1/2$" (1.3 cm) wide and affix to the top of each tag. Insert the finished tag into the pocket.

6 Weave the ribbon through the slits in the pockets and secure the ends with an adhesive glue dot.

7 Thread a piece of twine or yarn through the paper loops on the top of the tags, pull taut, and knot. This will form a dome on the top of the package.

8 Add a bow made from matching ribbon to the top of the package.

Cards with a Message

In the hands of a paper crafter, adhesive CD pockets will never again be used for their intended purpose! We see these versatile pockets used in journals, scrapbooks, and craft projects, as well as for cards and gift wrap. This card and envelope technique is a tribute to our well-known paper artist friend and teacher Mindy Carpenter, who inspires us to make custom envelopes in every size and pattern.

MATERIALS

- envelope to open and use as template
- heavy card stock
- adhesive CD pocket
- set of illustrated ABC stickers
- button
- decorative tape
- ink pads
- glue stick

TOOLS

- basic tool kit (see page 10)
- decorative-edge scissors

INSTRUCTIONS

Making the Envelope

1. Carefully open the seams of an envelope of the size you wish to duplicate.

2. Flatten out the paper and trace around the edges onto cardstock.

3. Cut out the envelope shape.

4. To make a lining for the envelope, cut the same shape in a contrasting pattern.

5. Glue the lining to the envelope, wrong sides together.

6. Use the original envelope as a guide for folding.

7. Glue the edges where they overlap.

8. Cut the edge of the envelope flap with decorative-edge scissors.

9. Use an ink pad to age the edges.

Making the Card

1. Use the size of your envelope to determine the size of the card.

2. Our envelope measures 7" x 11$^{1}/_{2}$" (17.8 x 29.2 cm) when closed. The card stock was cut to measure 12" x 9$^{1}/_{2}$" (30.5 x 24.1 cm), then folded horizontally to fit inside.

3. Mount an image (we used an alphabet sticker) onto the card stock cut $^{1}/_{2}$" (1.3 cm) larger on all sides. Mount this piece on a 4" x 4" (10.2 x 10.2 cm) square of card stock and place inside the adhesive CD pocket.

4. Embellish with a button and decorative tape around the pocket and on the card.

FOLD, CUT, AND WRAP

Gift Garlands

In another twist on the garland theme, use your paper-doll cutting experience to fashion a paper garland to encircle your gift boxes. The supplies you need are paper, glue, and scissors.

Experiment with anything from newspaper to flocked wallpaper and from colored card stock to rolls of gift wrap. Even if your efforts don't wind up on a package, this is valuable paper cutting "therapy."

We layered the black bow garland against patterned paper to make it "pop." And, if you only have paper enough to get three or four images from each fold, attach them together with tape. When you wrap it around the box, it will appear to be all one piece.

When you don't have just the right ribbon, you can always substitute a paper garland or just a contrasting strip of paper. Then again, you can use this idea along with ribbon for that "over-the-top" style that makes receiving a gift so special.

MATERIALS

- decorative paper
- glue

TOOLS

- basic tool kit (see page 10)

INSTRUCTIONS

1 Cut a strip of paper to the desired length, then accordion-fold the paper. While the paper is still folded, trace the main design on top.

2 Cut around the main design, making sure that some sections on the folds remain uncut; that will keep the garland in one piece.

3 Attach the garland to the package with double-sided tape. For added dimension, attach the garland to the package with double-sided photo-mounting tape.

Leftovers

Small scraps of paper and some basic supplies can turn into mini-masterpieces with a little time... and lots of imagination.

Get It in Writing

No need to ever have a generic pen when you can add this decorative touch (and you can pass secret messages in them too!).

① Remove the barrel and cut a $1/2$" (1.3 cm) strip of decorative paper to the length of the ink cartridge.

② Wrap the piece of decorative paper tightly around the ink cartridge and slide it back inside the pen.

It's a Wrap

Sweet and simple—this little box holds all things small and wonderful.

① Wrap decorative paper around a matchbox so that the drawer can still be opened.

② Use scraps of card stock for the top and bottom panels, and trim with decorative scissors.

③ Decorate the top panel and wrap a coordinating ribbon around the drawer to keep it from opening.

3

A Good Match

Keep a little tin of mini clothespins with your supplies. With a little scrap of paper and a leftover sticker you can quickly finish off a plain store-bought gift bag with a personal flair.

① Fold up the bottom 1/2" (1.3 cm) of a strip of card stock, tuck a square of vellum into this fold, and secure with a staple.

② Use rub-on letters for the outside of the matchbox and add a sticker flower to embellish a personal message inside.

③ Use a sticker-embellished mini clothespin to attach to a gift bag or package.

Studio Tip

Store your paper scraps according to color. When you need an embellishment for a card, tag, or package, take three to five pieces in the same color range and stack them from largest on the bottom to smallest on top. Place a decorative button in the center and sew the whole stack together with waxed linen thread. Affix to the card, tag, or box with double-stick tape or adhesive dots.

TEMPLATES

Luggage Tag Template (page 19)

Small Luggage Tag Template (page 24)

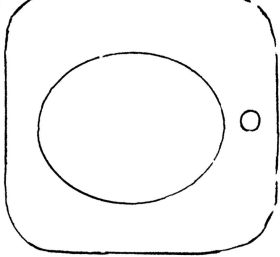

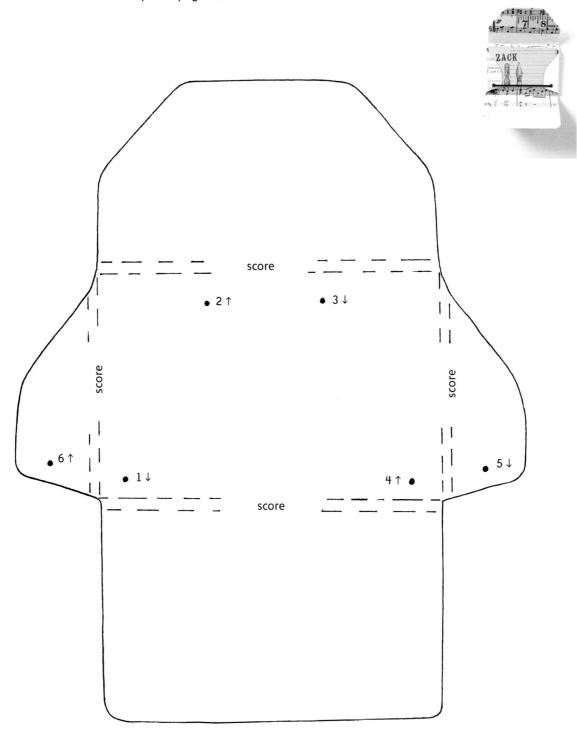

score

score

• 2 ↑   • 3 ↓

score   score

• 6 ↑

• 1 ↓   4 ↑ •   • 5 ↓

score

Tab Template (page 37)

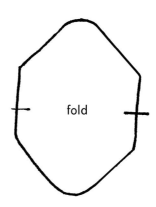

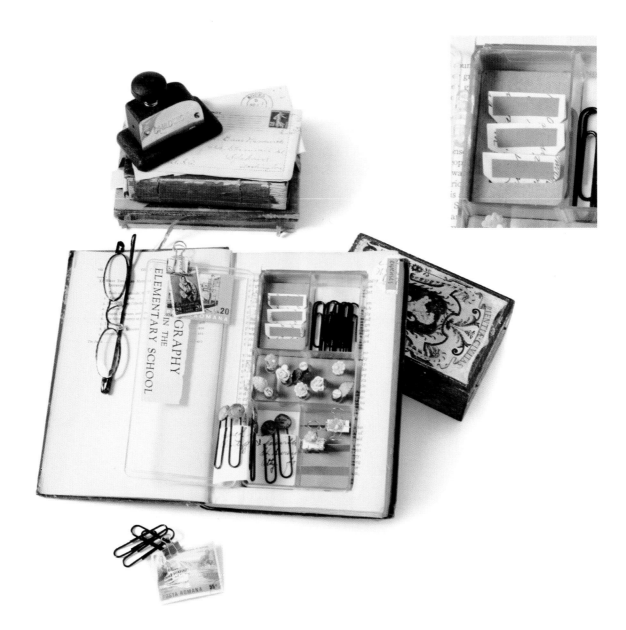

Napkin Ring Template (page 44)

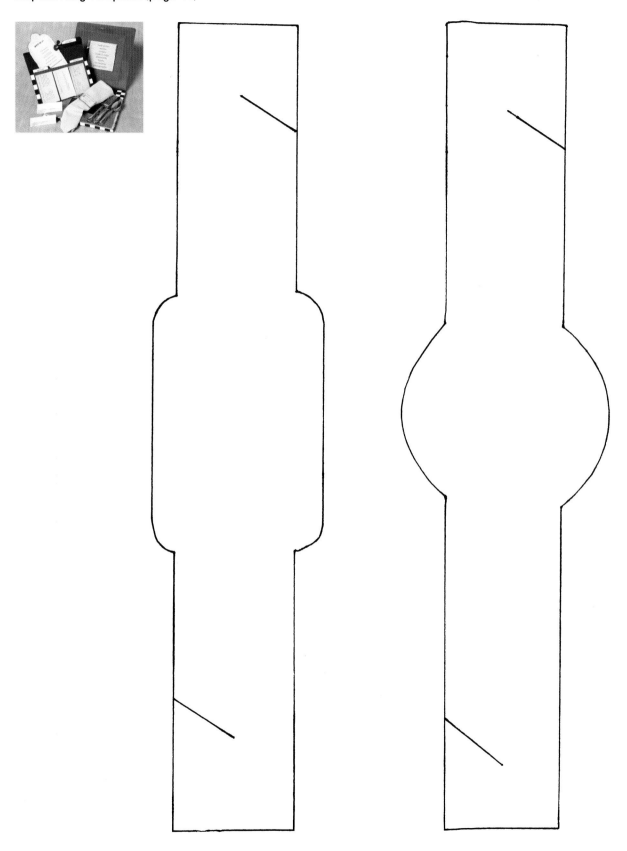

Menu Template (page 44)

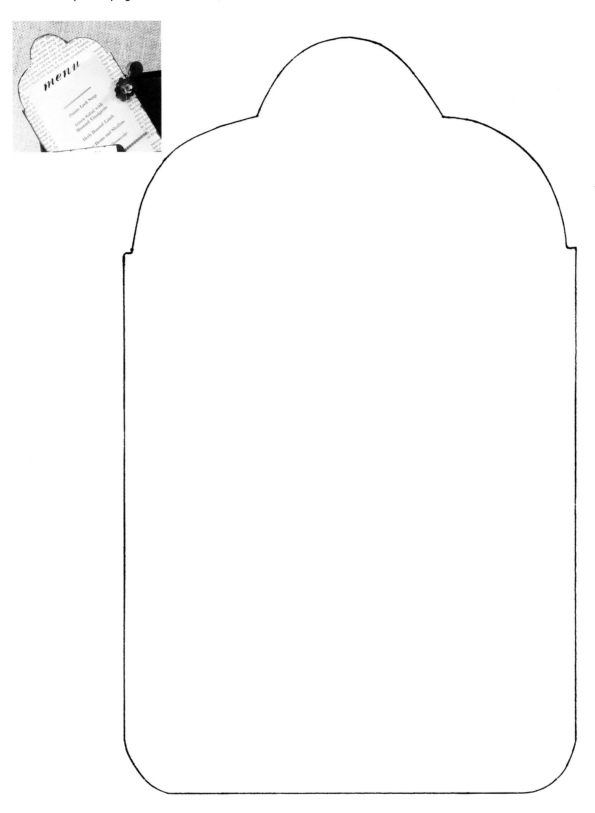

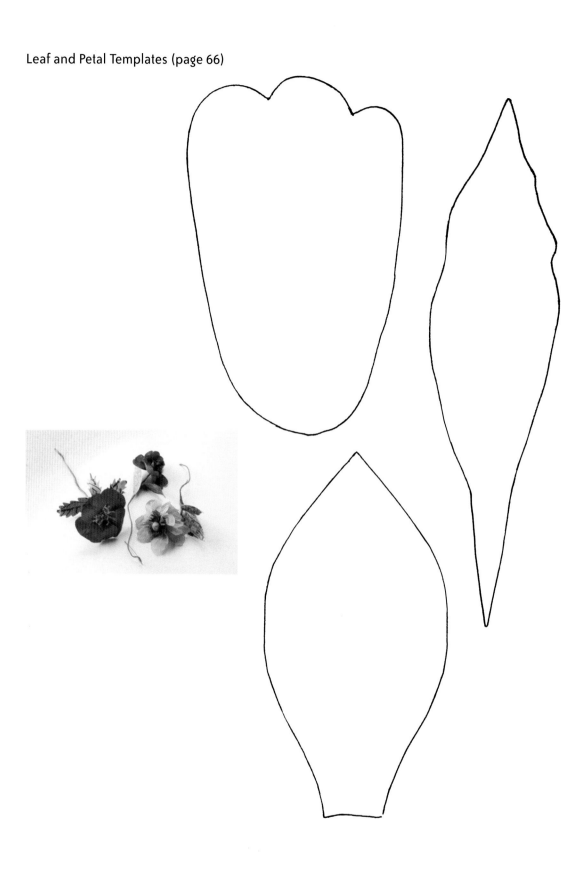

Embroidery Template (page 75)

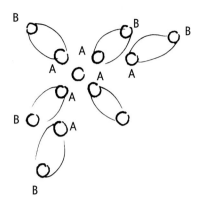

Button Book Template (page 75)

Pennant Templates (page 94)

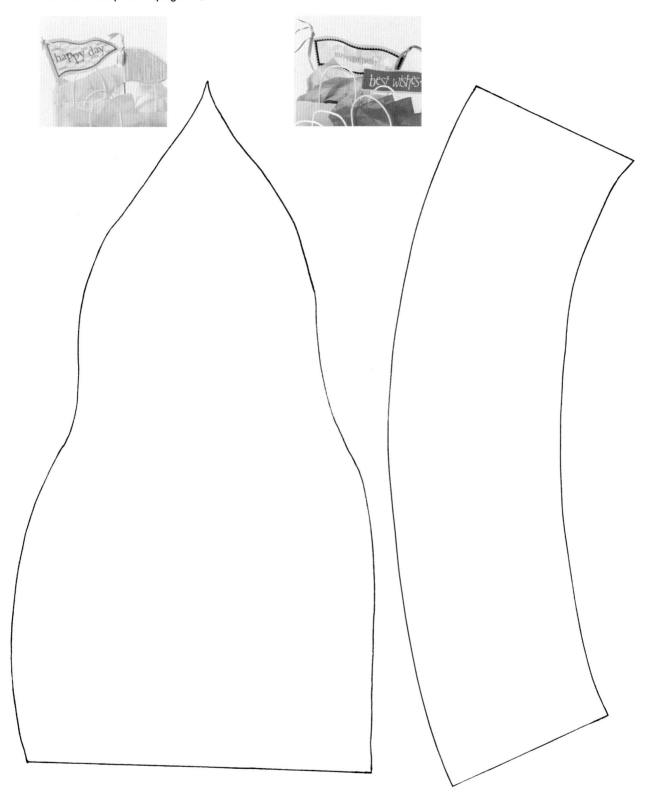

Pennant Templates (page 94)

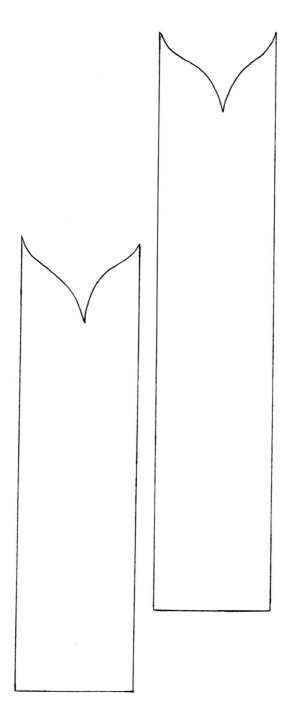

CLIP ART

This collection of clip art images is from The Mixed Mediums'
flea market adventures, grandma's library, vintage stores, and their
private stash. They will be useful for making some of the gifts
featured in the book or for your own versions of handmade gifts,
cards, tags, and accessories.

Passport

Rational Typewriting

MEDAL OF HONOR EDITION

HIGHEST AWARD AT THE PANAMA–PACIFIC INTERNATIONAL EXPOSITION

BY

RUPERT P. SoRELLE

AND IDA McLENAN CUTLER

COMPLETELY REWRITTEN, RE-ARRANGED
AND ADAPTED BY RUPERT P. SoRELLE
TO A SHORT, INTENSIVE COURSE

Copyright, 1917, by The Gregg Publishing Company
J53-F-10

The Gregg Publishing Company

NEW YORK   BOSTON   CHICAGO   SAN FRANCISCO   LONDON

Vintage Button Board

Recipe for Rabbit Stew

Vintage Label

Recipe for Rabbit Stew

any remaining flour mixture from the bag, and the onion. Allow to sauté slightly, then add ½ cup of the water. Cover and simmer gently until done. Add remaining ¼ cup water as needed. Rabbit should be very tender when done (about 1 hr). If more gravy is desired, the amount of liquid and flour may be increased after the rabbit is thoroughly done and removed from the pan. 3 to 4 servings.

RABBIT HASH

A good looking and delicious way to serve leftover rabbit

1½ to 2 cups chopped cooked rabbit
⅓ cup bacon drippings *or* shortening
3 medium baking potatoes, 1¼ lbs

3 medium onions, 6 oz
½ tsp celery salt
¼ tsp salt
Fresh ground black pepper

Remove meat from rabbit bones, and cut into small pieces with kitchen scissors or knife. Put drippings into skillet. Pare potatoes and grate coarsely. Slide potatoes into heated drippings; grate onion and add to potatoes; add rabbit and seasoning. Cover and cook moderately fast until potatoes are beautifully browned on under side. Stir to blend, turn over, cover again, and brown on under side. Cooking requires about 10 min in all. 4 servings.

JUGGED RABBIT

1 dressed rabbit, 1¾ lbs
3 cups cold water
2 tsp salt
¼ cup flour
¼ cup lard
2 egg-size onions
1/16 tsp black pepper
Dash of cayenne

2 slices lemon, ⅛-inch thick
2 chicken bouillon cubes in
2 cups hot water
2 tbsp flour
2½ lbs baking potatoes, pared, cut as for French Fries
½ tsp salt

Start oven 10 min before baking; set to mod (350° F).

Clean rabbit, p 745. Cut in serving pieces and place in bowl. Mix water and salt, pour over rabbit; turn small plate over to weigh down and let stand 20 min. Drain. Place on absorbent paper and pat dry. Roll each piece in flour. Heat lard in heavy skillet, brown rabbit on both sides well and cook slowly about 15 min. Remove to baking dish and add onion and lemon slices with rind removed and potatoes. Drain fat from skillet leaving about 2 tbsp, add flour, stir to keep smooth and slowly add bouillon-water mixture. Cook until gravy is slightly thickened. Pour over rabbit, cover and bake 45 min or until meat and potatoes are tender, 1½ to 2 hrs. 4 servings.

PRODUCT MANUFACTURERS BY PROJECT

Each project in this book is listed here by page number to help you locate manufacturers for most of the supplies used. To locate more information about a specific manufacturer see most of, page 120–123.

Page 14, Traveling Light: The Perfect Handmade Journal
heavyweight paper, blank book, glassine envelope, ribbon, blank postcards, postage stamps, map, rub-on letters (Creative Imaginations)

Page 16, Your Passport Please: Document Holder
heavy paper to match journal, tissue paper, brads (Making Memories), waxed string (Scrapworks), plastic sleeve, rub-on letters (Creative Imaginations), hook and loop tape

Page 19, Nothing to Declare: Luggage Tag
handmade or purchased heavy paper, acetate transparency (3M), plain-colored card stock (Prism), post and screw fastener

Page 20, Frequent Flier: Traveling Artist Portfolio
purchased portfolio measuring 12 1/2" x 9 1/2" (31.8 x 24.1 cm) (Staples), map of destination, spiral-bound sketchbook, string and button envelope, black elastic, decorative brads (Making Memories), black acrylic paint, paintbrushes, watercolor paper, clear plastic adhesive-back container (3M), colored pencils (Carta Products)

Page 29, Magnetic Personality: Metal Message Board
vintage papers, decorative papers (Anna Griffin), collage items such as mailbox stickers, wooden letters, old rulers, magnetic clips, or brass charms (Fancifuls, Inc.), ribbons, magnets, metal roof flashing, clear epoxy stickers (Making Memories), soft gel (Golden), thinned acrylic paints or glazes (Golden), glue stick (3M), strong, fast-drying liquid glue (3M)

Page 30 Collage Under Glass: Paperweights
card stock (Prism), decorative velvet paper (SEI), small trinkets and paper ephemera, glue stick (3M), fast-drying liquid glue (3M)

Page 33, Calling All Cards: Business Card Holder
decorative papers (Anna Griffin), eyelets, elastic cord, glue stick (3M)

Page 37, Classy Office Supplies: New Use for an Old Book
card stock (Prism), decorative paper or paper ephemera, vintage book, pushpins, paper clips, binder clips, corrugated cardboard, small paper flowers and leaves (Paper Source), white shrink plastic (Lucky Squirrel), plastic box (Container Store), glue stick (3M), pigment or permanent ink (Colorbox, Tsukineko), soft gel (Golden), clear dimensional glaze (Judi Kins)

Page 44, Chef's Collection: Kitchen Journal
trifold portfolio (Staples), blank recipe cards, acetate transparency (3M), chalkboard paint (Lowes), file folders (Costco), metal drawer handle and knobs (Lowes), handwritten recipes, personal photographs of food, decorative papers (Rubbermaid), pages from old cookbooks, gesso (Golden), iridescent stainless steel acrylic (Golden), CD case, hook and loop tape, aluminum (Art Emboss), library pockets

Page 49, Arty-Chokes: Kitschy Culinary Art
faux artichokes, printed tissue paper, printed ephemera (old books and maps), small embellishments (brass charms, game pieces, ribbon scraps), small letter stickers or letter die cuts (QuiKutz), permanent markers (Sanford), glue stick (3M), fast-drying liquid glue (3M), permanent inks (Tsukineko)

Page 50, Recipe Management: Stylish Clipboards
small clipboards, decorative paper (Anna Griffin, Creative Imaginations), ribbon, library pocket, vintage recipe, chalk, waxed twine (Scrapworks), brads (Karen Foster), black chalkboard paint, cardboard, drawer knobs and washers, bolts and wing nuts, heat shrink tubing, rubber stamps (Personal Stamp Exchange), ink pads, label sticker (7 Gypsies), rub-on letters (Making Memories)

Page 58, East Meets West: Origami Writing Set
decorative paper (NRN Designs), envelopes, card stock (Prism)

Page 62, Flea Market Style: French Flower Buckets
white poster board, wallpaper, decorative paper (Creative Imaginations), vintage label, acrylic paint, gesso (Golden), double-stick tape (3M), clear adhesive dots (Therm O Web), wire for the handle, silver spray paint (Krylon), silver foil pen (Krylon), pom-pom fringe

Page 66, Perfect Posies: Paper Flowers
solid color papers, decorative papers, crepe paper, green florist wire, green florist tape, spray glue or paper glue (3M), glue dots (Therm O Web), gold foil pen (Krylon)

Page 71 Designs from Nature: Journal Necklace
brass locket (Fancifuls, Inc.), decorative paper (Anna Griffin), permanent ink (Tsukineko), rub-ons (Creative Imaginations), old postage stamps, rhinestone stickers (Making Memories), beads, jump rings, cotton or leather cord, jewelry crimp ends, lobster clasp, decorative-edge scissors (Fiskars)

Page 75, A Best Seller: The Button Book
buttons, decorative card stock (Making Memories), thin cardboard, ribbon, small ribbon buckle (Making Memories), brads (Making Memories), rickrack (Making Memories), permanent pen (Sanford), glassine envelope, sticker sheet (Avery), stapler (Swingline), felt scrap, sewing kit, giant metal ring (Paper Source), small plastic bags, glue stick (3M), foam adhesive (3M), fast-drying liquid glue (3M), die cutter and alphabet dies (QuiKutz), decorative-edge scissors (Fiskars)

Page 82, Beautifully Composed: Composition-Book Cards
decorative paper (Anna Griffin, Creative Imaginations), card stock (Prism), small composition book (Norcom, Inc), coin envelope (Staples), ribbon, watercolor paper, stamps or other ephemera, decorative paper clips (Scrapworks, 7 Gypsies), glue stick (3M), colored markers (EK Success)

Page 86, The Big Easy: 20-Minute Cards
card stock (Prism), paint chips, decorative paper, envelopes, three-dimensional stickers (EK Success), ribbon, glue stick (3M), small die-cut tags (QuiKutz)

Page 88, Pick a Tag, Any Tag: Gift Tag Folios
card stock (Prism), decorative paper (Anna Griffin, Creative Imaginations, SEI), mat boards, elastic cord, eyelets, ribbons and fibers, buckle (optional), glue stick (3M), removable tape (3M)

Page 92, Showing Your Sentiments: A Word Garland
card stock, C-Thru ruler, decorative paper (SEI, Creative Imaginations), eyelets, brads, pebbles, ribbon, twine, or fibers, rub-on letters and words (Heidy Swapp, Making Memories), die-cut letters (QuiKutz), paper flowers (Prima), rhinestones

Page 94, Rah! Rah! Rah!: Gift Bag Pennants
decorative paper (Anna Griffin, Creative Imaginations), decorative-edge scissors (Fiskars), rub-ons (Scrapworks), die cuts (QuiKutz), stickers, tags, ribbon, markers (EK Success)

Page 97, Supreme Makeover: Well-Dressed Office Supplies
box, decorative wrapping paper, adhesive CD pockets (Smead), decorative paper (Anna Griffin, Cavellini), card stock (Prism), ribbon approximately 1 1/2" (3.8 cm) wide, twine or yarn, rub-on letters (Scrapworks)

Page 98, Purposeful Pockets: Cards with a Message
set of illustrated ABC stickers (Cavellini), button, decorative tape (Heidi Swapp), colored ink pads

Page 101, Fold, Cut, and Wrap: Gift Garlands
decorative paper, fibers

OUT AND ABOUT WITH THE MIXED MEDIUMS

During the process of writing *Handmade Gifts*, The Mixed Mediums realized there were times when we had to close our laptops, peel the gel medium off our fingers, and hit the road for a field trip. These are some of the stores that enchanted, excited, and inspired us. Many are small, one-of-a-kind places where you can chat with the owner about their merchandise, art philosophy, and nearby restaurants for lunch. Others are large, national stores that may not be as cozy and personal but offer dazzling displays and the latest in innovative paper goods. Either way, it is all about the experience of shopping as much as it is about acquiring materials.

With a few clicks on your computer, you can take a look at our favorite stores from tiny towns on the California coast, to the boulevards of Paris and the winding side streets of Florence. The larger, nationwide stores have catalogs. Order one when you visit the website and you will be delighted each time one shows up in your mailbox.

Resources

UNITED STATES

Anthropologie: *a nationwide home accessories and clothing store that always incorporates paper art in its merchandising displays. Quirky, clever, and always something new*
www.anthropologie.com

Archiver's: *lovely memory, scrapbook, and paper art stores throughout the Midwest*
www.archiversonline.com

The ARTbar: *mixed-media art studio and retail store in an exquisite historical building*
Santa Ana, CA
714.558.2445
www.theartbar.net

French General: *elegant ephemera, antique buttons, notions, beads and ribbon—all from antique fairs in the south of France*
Hollywood, CA
323.462.0818
www.frenchgeneral.com

Hobby Lobby Creative Centers: *general crafts and hobby supplies*
www.hobbylobby.com

Jennifer Price Studio: *an ever-changing assemblage of handcrafted functional art*
At SoLo in Solana Beach, CA
858.794.9016
www.jenniferpricestudio.com

Jo-Ann Stores: *fabrics and crafts and all the basics*
www.joann.com

Kate's Paperie: *beautiful paper boutique with locations around New York City*
www.katespaperie.com

Lucky Paperie: *letterpress designs, journals, memory books, albums, and paper*
Pasadena, CA
626.440.9440
www.luckypaperie.com

Michael's: *national chain of craft and art supply stores—where to go to find the basics*
800.MICHAELS
www.michaels.com

Paper Source: *these stores throughout the United States are a delight for paper lovers. We spend hours looking at the books, displays samples, and handmade papers. Request their catalog when you check out the website*
www.paper-source.com

Paperie: *a sumptuous assortment of handmade papers and journals*
San Diego, CA
619.234.5457

Paris to the Moon: *paper artists reign in this store that is like stepping back in time to the Victorian era*
Costa Mesa, CA
949.642.0942
For a preview of their magical merchandise visit:
www.studiodsharp.com
www.fgandcompany.com

ReCollections: *Michael's-owned stores devoted to papercraft and scrapbooking*
www.recollectionsonline.com

Ruby Lang: *antiquities, oddities, and wearable paper extravaganzas*
At SoLo in Solana Beach, CA
858.794.9016

Sterling Art: *another paper paradise for excellent art supplies and museum quality paper for replicating artwork*
800.953.2953
www.sterlingart.com

Target: *design for the masses, and lovely supplies for paper art and more*
www.target.com

Australia

Eckersley's Arts, Crafts, and Imagination
(store locations in New South Wales, Queensland, South Australia, and Victoria)
phone for catalog: 61.1.300.657.766
www.eckersleys.com.au

Canada

Curry's Art Store
Ontario, Canada
art and craft supplies
800.268.2969
www.currys.com

Lazar Studiowerx Inc
British Columbia, Canada
rubber stamps, art tools
866.478.9379
www.lazarstudiowerx.com

France

Jen Bitto has spent hours researching paper stores in Paris and allotted an entire day to check them out. Take an armchair vacation to the City of Lights by visiting the websites provided showing Jen's favorite shops.

Calligrane
4-6 Rue du Pont Louis Phillipe
Paris, France

Graphigro
art supplies
6e arrondissement
133, Rue De Rennes
Paris, France
www.graphigro.com
33.01.53.36000

L'Art du Papier
48 Rue Vavin
Paris, France
www.art-du-papier.fr

Marie Papier
26 Rue Vavin
Paris, France
www.mariepapier.com

Papier +
9 rue du Pont Louis Philippe
Paris, France
www.papierplus.com

Italy

Italians have been making the world's most beautiful paper for hundreds of years. Perhaps that is why they don't feel the need to establish websites! These are Linda's favorite paper stores in Florence. They may not be on the web but you will find them all within walking distance of the Duomo.

Carteria Tassotti, Via Dei Servi 9/11r

Il Papiro, Via Cavour, 55r

Rigacci, Via Dei Servi 7

Et Cetera. Via Della Vigna Nuova 82/r

And, when in Rome, spend some time at Fabriano, the famous Italian paper company. They actually have a well-stocked and beautiful store at the Rome airport, of all places. This is a paper aficionado's idea of what every airport should offer at the departure gates!

New Zealand

Littlejohns Art & Graphic Supplies Ltd.
170 Victoria Street
Wellington, New Zealand
64.04.385.2099

United Kingdom

T N Lawrence & Son Ltd.
208 Portland Road
Hove UK BN3 5QT
44.0845.644.3232
www.lawrence.co.uk

Creative Crafts
11 The Square
Winchester,
Hampshire, UK SO23 9ES
44.01962.856266
www.creativecrafts.co.uk

HobbyCraft Group Limited
art and craft supplies
7 Enterprise Way
Aviation Park
Bournemouth International Airport
Christchurch
Dorset, UK BH23 6HG
44.01202.596100
www.hobbycraft.co.uk

John Lewis
(stores throughout the UK)
Flagship Store
Oxford Street
London W1A 1EX
44.01207.629.7711
www.johnlewis.co.uk

FLEA MARKETS AND ANTIQUE SHOWS

Jenn Mason's yearly trek to the famous Brimfield Antique & Collectible has become a tradition that garners her one-of-a-kind embellishments, ephemera, and a chance to spend the day with her East Coast girlfriends.

www.brimfieldshow.com

www.shortcitybreak.co.uk
European flea markets locator

www.fleamarketguide.com
State by state listing of markets in the United States

www.discoverfrance.net
Listings of France's best flea markets

Product Resources

Website and/or contact information is provided below for products used in this book. Many of these company websites either allow you to order directly (and ship internationally) or list stores where their products are available.

3M
www.3m.com
Adhesives including glue sticks, specialty tapes, foam tape squares, and spray adhesives. Also transparencies and laminating supplies

7 Gypsies
www.7gypsies.com
Scrapbooking supplies including unusual embellishments

Anna Griffin, Inc.
www.annagriffin.com
Fine decorative paper and embellishments for scrapbooking and paper arts

Avery
www.avery.com
Office tags and supplies

Carta Products
www.cartaproducts.com
Colored pencil sets

Cavallini
www.cavallini.com
Fine Italian decorative papers and accessories

Clearsnap
www.clearsnap.com
Ink and rubber stamp manufacturer including stamp wheels

Container Store (The)
www.thecontainerstore.com
Organizational supplies and gift wrap

Costco
www.costco.com
Superstore for home goods

Creative Imaginations
www.cigift.com
Scrapbook papers, supplies, and embellishments

EK Success
www.eksuccess.com
Scrapbook papers, supplies, and embellishments

Fancifuls, Inc.
www.fancifulsinc.com
Brass charms and embellishments

Fiskars
www.fiskars.com
Scissors and cutting implements

Glue Dots International
www.gluedotsinternational.com
Adhesive dots for paper craft applications

Golden Paints
www.goldenpaints.com
Quality line of paints, fluid acrylics, and mediums for art

Judi Kins
www.judikins.com
Stamps and supplies including Diamond Glaze

K & Co.
www.kandcompany.com
Scrapbook paper, albums, and embellishments

Krylon
www.krylon.com
Paints and painting products

Lowe's
www.lowes.com
Hardware supplies

Lucky Squirrel
www.luckysquirrel.com
Shrink plastic supplies

Making Memories
www.makingmemories.com
Scrapbook paper, tools, supplies, and embellishments

Norcom, Inc.
www.norcominc.com
Mini composition books

Paper Source
www.paper-source.com
Paper for paper art and scrapbooking

Prism
www.prismpapers.com
Large selection of fine card stocks for paper crafting, including exclusive textured line

Provo Craft
www.provocraft.com
Craft supplies

QuicKutz
www.quickutz.com
Die-cut machine and unique alphabet and shaped dies

ReadySet
www.readysettools.com
Unique eyelet setting tool that can be used anywhere

Rubbermaid
www.rubbermaid.com
Makers of plastic storage and Con-Tact paper

Sanford
www.sanford.com
Maker of Sharpie markers

Supply Contributors

Special thanks to the following manufacturers for contributing their products for use in this book. We encourage you to look into these companies and their wonderful products.

Scrapworks
www.scrapworks.com
Scrapbook paper, tools, supplies, and embellishments

SEI
www.shopsei.com
Scrapbook paper and supplies

Smead
www.smead.com
Producer of filing and records management products

Staples
www.staples.com
Office and paper supplies

Swingline
www.swingline.com
Staplers and supplies

Therm O Web
www.thermoweb.com
Adhesive (Zots)

Tsukineko
www.tsukineko.com
Ink for rubber stamping and paper art

X-Acto
www.hunt-corp.com
X-Acto knives and blades

3M
St. Paul, MN 55144 USA
888.3M.HELPS (364.3577)
www.3m.com

American Tag
800.223.3956
www.americantag.net
Manufacturer of the HomePro heavy-duty hole punch, and eyelet, rivet, nail head, metal corner, snap, and rhinestone setter

Anna Griffin Inc.
733 Lambert Drive
Atlanta, GA 30324 USA
888.817.8170
www.annagriffin.com
Scrapbook papers and embellishments

Cavallini
401 Forbes Boulevard
South San Francisco, CA 94080 USA
800.226.5287
www.cavallini.com
Paper products

The C-Thru Ruler Company
6 Britton Drive
Bloomfield, CT 06002 USA
800.243.8419
www.cthruruler.com
Cutting-edge innovator and international leader in measurement and art materials

Fiskars
2537 Daniels Street
Madison, WI 53718 USA
866.348.5661
www.fiskars.com
www.fiskarscrafts.com

Golden
188 Bell Road
New Berlin, NY 13411-9527 USA
800.959.6543
www.goldenpaints.com
Professional quality art materials that extend creative opportunities for artists and strengthen industry standards

Heidi Swapp
Advantus Corporation
12276 San Jose Boulevard
Building 115
Jacksonville, FL 32223 USA
904.482.0092
www.heidiswapp.com
Scrapbook papers and embellishments

May Arts
203.637.5285 (fax)
sales@mayarts.com
www.mayarts.com
Beautiful ribbons for crafting, sewing, and decorating

Prism
P.O. Box 25068
Salt Lake City UT 84125 USA
866.901.1002
www.prismpapers.com
Scrapbooking papers

QuicKutz, Inc.
1365 West 1250 South
Suite 100
Orem, UT 84058 USA
888.702.1146
www.quickutz.com
Portable, accessible die-cutting

Scrapworks, Inc.
3038 Specialty Circle
Suite C
Salt Lake City, UT 84115 USA
801.363.1010
www.scrapworks.com
Scrapbook papers and embellishments

Tsukineko
17640 NE 65th Street
Redmond, WA 98052 USA
425.883.7733
425.883.7418 (fax)
sales@tsukineko.com
www.tsukineko.com
Fine-quality inks and ink pads for your crafting projects

ABOUT THE AUTHORS

The Mixed Mediums perusing the selection of ephemera at L.A.'s French General:
(left to right) Jennifer Francis Bitto, Jenn Mason, and Linda Blinn.

JENNIFER FRANCIS BITTO, former editor and stylist of *Take Ten, The Stampers' Sampler,* and *Inspirations,* represents the artist and crafter looking for quick and easy projects that make a big impact. Her work has appeared in various crafting magazines, in addition to her Mixed Medium coauthored books. She makes her home in Vista, California, where she works assisting an executive coach, and as a consultant to industry companies. This is her first book.

LINDA BLINN is a writer, editor, teacher, designer, and artist. She is a magazine editor who enjoys exploring current art trends and interviewing prominent artists and authors. She is the author of *Making Family Journals* (Quarry Books, 2006). Her artwork has also appeared in magazines including *Victoria, Cloth Paper Scissors,* and *Somerset Studio* as well as three books: *Artists' Journals and Sketchbooks* by Lynne Perrella, *Pockets, Pullouts and Hiding Places* by Jenn Mason, and *Beyond Scrapbooks* by Barbara Bourassa. She teaches at retail stores and artist's conventions and has appeared on the DIY Network. She lives in the small coastal town of San Clemente, California.

JENN MASON is a fine artist, writer, teacher, and product designer who loves a new challenge. Her work has appeared in many books including *Pockets, Pullouts, and Hiding Places* (Quarry Books, 2005). She enjoys teaching women across the country and abroad through her writing and classes. Jenn also spends her time designing products for the paper art industry and consulting to companies within the industry. The rest of her free time is joyfully absorbed by her two young daughters and husband. While she and her family have lived in Colorado and Texas, they currently call Boston, Massachusetts, home.

ACKNOWLEDGMENTS

No book could have been completed without the exceptional patience of my roommate and partner in crime, Ernie. My greatest thanks for his wordless acceptance of my piles and for sacrificing more than a few surfaces for just one more of my creative whirlwinds. And to my Mixed Medium muses, your talent and artistic spirits shall always be cherished. —JB

Author Kate Millet said, "You have to be a little patient if you are an artist, people don't always get you the first time." I think this quote applies to artists who write books as well. I thank all of you who "got me" the first time. —LB

A special thanks to the sweetest little girls who patiently wait for Mommy to send "just one more email." I hope one day we can write a book together! Thanks also to my manager, head shrink, and muse, a.k.a. Matt—I owe you one. —JM

LOOKING FOR MORE FROM THE MIXED MEDIUMS' PAPER ART WORKSHOP?

Available January 2007

Paper Art Workshop
CELEBRATING BABY
Personalized Projects for Moms, Memories, and Gear

Whether you're a mother, grandmother, aunt, or girlfriend, *Celebrating Baby* offers an assortment of wonderful handmade gifts to celebrate the birth of a child in style! This lovely book features an exquisite collection of beautiful handmade paper baby gifts that can be personalized any way you like. The projects include mobiles, wall decorations, photo frames, brag books, baby books, announcements, a growth chart, a retro memory case, and even a stylish diaper bag ensemble. You'll learn how to turn precious photos into a crystal memory bracelet, and how to create a heritage chandelier. Learn simple techniques and expert "studio" tips that will take your passion for beautiful paper to the next level.